Microcomputers and Exceptional Children

Microcomputers and Exceptional Children

Randy Elliot Bennett and Charles A. Maher
Co-Editors

The Haworth Press
New York

Microcomputers and Exceptional Children has also been published as *Special Services in the Schools,* Volume 1, Number 1, Fall 1984.

© 1984 by The Haworth Press, Inc. All rights reserved. No part of this work may be reproduced or utilized in any form or by any means, electronic or mechanical, including photocopying, microfilm and recording, or by any information storage and retrieval system, without permission in writing from the publisher. Printed in the United States of America.

The Haworth Press, Inc., 28 East 22 Street, New York, NY 10010

Library of Congress Cataloging in Publication Data
Main entry under title:

Microcomputers and exceptional children.

   "Also published as Special services in the schools, Volume 1, Number 1, Fall 1984"—Verso t.p.
   Includes bibliographies.
   1. Handicapped children—Education—Data processing—Addresses, essays, lectures. 2. Computer-assisted instruction—Addresses, essays, lectures. 3. Microcomputers—Addresses, essays, lectures. I. Bennett, Randy Elliot, 1940- . II. Maher, Charles A., 1944- .
LC4024.M53   1984   371.9'043   84-10784
ISBN 0-86656-297-4

Microcomputers and Exceptional Children

Special Services in the Schools
Volume 1, Number 1

CONTENTS

Introduction to *Special Services in the Schools* Charles A. Maher	1
Microcomputers and Exceptional Children: An Overview Randy Elliot Bennett Charles A. Maher	3
Computer-Based Assessment of Special-Needs Students Ted S. Hasselbring	7
Computer-Based Assessment of Special-Needs Children: Current Developments	8
Expert Systems: The Future of Computer-Based Assessment?	15
Summary	18
The Microcomputer as Perceptual Tool: Searching for Systematic Learning Strategies With Handicapped Infants Richard P. Brinker	21
The Role of the Microcomputer in Special Services	23
Microcomputer as Perceptual Tool	24
Artificial Intelligence and Expert Systems	33

Instructional Uses of Microcomputers With Elementary Aged Mildly Handicapped Children   **37**
    Joseph K. Torgesen

  Effectiveness of Computer Assisted Instruction With Young Children   38
  Remaining Questions   40
  Priorities for Use of Computers   41
  Programs Currently Available in Reading and Math   43
  Needs for the Present and Future   46

Microcomputer Technology and Related Services   **49**
    Roland K. Yoshida

  Description of Microcomputer Adaptations   51
  Cost/Benefit Analysis and Microcomputer Innovations   55
  Conclusion   59

Training Special Education Personnel for Effective Use of Microcomputer Technology: Critical Needs and Directions   **63**
    Melvyn I. Semmel
    Merith A. Cosden
    Dorothy S. Semmel
    Eve Kelemen

  Factors Influencing Teacher Utilization of Technology   66
  Teacher Effectiveness and Effective Microcomputer Instruction: Considerations for Teacher Training   74
  Recommendations for Teacher Training: A Two-Tiered Approach   77

Evaluating Microcomputer Programs   **83**
    Randy Elliot Bennett

  Review the Program's Design   84
  Review the Program's Operation   86
  Review the Program's Outcomes   87
  Conclusion   89

**Assessing and Facilitating School Readiness
for Microcomputers**   **91**
    Robert J. Illback
    Linda Hargan

Organizational Readiness for an Innovation	92
Case Illustration of Organizational Readiness Factors	95
Operationalizing Organizational Readiness	99
Conclusion	104

**Using Microcomputers for Administrative Purposes:
Suggestions for Development and Management**   **107**
    David L. Hayden

Ways Microcomputers Can Assist Administration	108
Developing and Managing Information Systems: Some Considerations for LEA Administrators	109
Developing Information Management Systems: Some Considerations for State Administrators	111
Conclusion	112

EDITOR

CHARLES A. MAHER, *Department of School Psychology, Graduate School of Applied and Professional Psychology, Rutgers University, Box 819, Piscataway, NJ 08854*

EDITORIAL ASSISTANT

LOUIS J. KRUGER, *Department of School Psychology, Graduate School of Applied and Professional Psychology, Rutgers University, Box 819, Piscataway, NJ*

EDITORIAL BOARD

MARTY ABRAMSON, *U.S. Department of Education*
ROBERT ALGOZZINE, *University of Florida*
JACK I. BARDON, *University of North Carolina-Greensboro*
RANDY ELLIOT BENNETT, *Educational Testing Service*
LEONARD BURRELLO, *Indiana University*
CARY CHERNISS, *Rutgers University*
KIM B. COLEMAN, *Morris-Union (NJ) Consortium*
VIRGINIA DIXON, *Intermediate School District #535, Rochester, MN*
JAMES F. DONOVAN, *West Orange (NJ) School District*
DAVID DRISCOLL, *Fairport (NY) Central School District*
NANCY ENELL, *San Juan (CA) Unified School District*
N. S. FAGLEY, *Rutgers University*
DONALD C. FLEMING, *Chesterfield County (VA) Schools*
SUSAN G. FORMAN, *University of South Carolina*
DAVID E. GREENBURG, *Indiana State Department of Education*
FRANK M. GRESHAM, *Louisiana State University*
JEFF GRIMES, *Iowa State Department of Public Instruction*
JERRY GROSS, *Long Beach (CA) Unified School District*
MARY KATHERINE HAWRYLUK, *South Brunswick (NJ) School District*
PATRICIA HEASTON, *Chicago Board of Education*
ROBERT J. ILLBACK, *Fort Knox (KY) Dependent Schools*
HENRY L. JANZEN, *University of Alberta*
LEONARD JASON, *DePaul University*
MICHAEL KABLER, *Ohio State School for the Blind*
BARBARA KEOGH, *University of California-Los Angeles*
THOMAS R. KRATOCHWILL, *University of Wisconsin-Madison*
GERALD M. KYSELA, *University of Alberta*
JEFFREY OSOWSKI, *New Jersey State Department of Education*
H. THOMPSON PROUT, *State University of New York at Albany*
THEODORE F. RIGGEN, *Joint Agreement District #802, Chicago Hgts., IL*
LUCINDA SEARES, *Howell Township (NJ) School District*
BETH SULZER-AZAROFF, *University of Massachusetts*
MELVYN I. SEMMEL, *University of California-Santa Barbara*
JOHN TAYLOR, *Boulder County (CO) Board for Developmental Disabilities*
ANN P. TURNBULL, *University of Kansas*
MILTON P. WILSON, *California State Department of Education*
JOSEPH E. ZINS, *University of Cincinnati*
ROLAND K. YOSHIDA, *Fordham University*
JAMES E. YSSELDYKE, *University of Minnesota*

Microcomputers and Exceptional Children

Introduction to
Special Services in the Schools

The delivery of special services to children and youth in school and related educational settings is a diverse, complex, multidisciplinary endeavor. The service delivery task is diverse because special services systems are comprised of many kinds of services: pre-placement evaluation, instructional programs, counseling and other forms of supportive assistance, staff development training and administrative policies and procedures. The delivery of special services is complex because of the diversity of programs that must be coordinated if maximum educational benefit to all students is to result. Last, special services delivery requires the contributions of professionals from many disciplines because of the wide variety of specialized needs of those students served by the system. Special services professionals include special and remedial education teachers; school counselors and psychologists; nurses and social workers; physical, occupational, and speech therapists; supervisors, directors, and administrators.

Because the delivery of special services is diverse, complex and multidisciplinary, professionals must constantly work to improve their knowledge of exceptional children and the most effective ways to serve them. To perform more effectively, professionals need information about current and future trends on delivering special services in the schools.

This issue launches *Special Services in the Schools,* a quarterly publication with an applied professional focus. Articles to be included in this multidisciplinary journal will be instructive and informative to all special services professionals employed in school and related educational settings. The articles are aimed at assisting professionals in performing such service delivery tasks as:

—assessing individual pupils and groups to determine their special educational needs

—designing individualized and group programs
—assisting regular and special classroom teachers to foster academic achievement and functional living of special students
—enhancing the social and emotional development of pupils through preventive and remedial approaches
—helping school administrators to develop smoothly functioning organizational systems
—fostering the physical well-being of special students
—involving parents and families in special programs
—education and training of school staff to more effectively educate special needs students

Various kinds of articles will be published in *Special Services in the Schools*. These articles will include reviews of applied educational research; descriptions of successful programs that are supported by empirical evidence; policy perspectives on current and future issues and trends; guidelines for planning, implementing, and evaluating programs; and book and other educational materials reviews. Periodically, special journal issues will be published on topics of contemporary relevance. For this journal volume, there are two such issues: the current issue, and the third issue which will focus on strategies for promotion of the physical and emotional well being of special needs students.

All articles to be published in *Special Services in the Schools* will be evaluated anonymously by the distinguished members of the Journal's Editorial Board, as well as by other expert reviewers, all of whom are knowledgeable about and experienced in special services delivery. These editorial reviews will provide information that authors will find helpful in revising and strengthening their manuscripts as well as useful for future publication efforts.

As Editor, I stand committed to disseminating timely, important, and relevant information. I welcome your manuscript submissions, ideas about special services delivery, and commentary on published articles.

Charles A. Maher
Editor

Microcomputers and Exceptional Children: An Overview

Randy Elliot Bennett
Charles A. Maher

In a recent book entitled *Planning and Evaluating Special Education Services* (Maher & Bennett, 1984), we pictured the special services delivery system as being composed of five parts: assessment, instruction, related services, personnel development, and administration. Each of these components was presented as working to directly or indirectly meet the educational needs of special children. Assessment was stated to focus upon gathering the data needed to make educational decisions about children. Instruction centered upon addressing the academic and social goals contained in pupils' individualized education programs. The supports needed to help children benefit from special education were provided by a range of related services including speech and occupational therapy and counseling. Personnel development served to assist school staff in developing and maintaining the skills needed to perform their jobs. Finally, the interaction of these service components was coordinated by administration.

These five components of special education are being rapidly and dramatically transformed. The largest single force behind this transformation is the microprocessor. This silicone chip contains the electronic instructions that form the heart of the personal computer and its many related devices. These related devices include voice synthesizers, graphics tablets, and voice recognition components.

The pages that follow detail the many ways in which the microcomputer and its relatives are changing the face of special education. In the lead paper, Hasselbring discusses the application of microcomputers to educational assessment. His paper introduces the notion of intelligent systems that will soon actively help the diagnostician to select, administer, and score tests, as well as interpret the results of assessment.

Following Hasselbring's paper is Brinker's presentation of the microcomputer as a tool for monitoring pupil progress and adjusting educational programs on the basis of monitoring information. Used in this way, Brinker sees the microcomputer as a means of bridging the perennial gap between assessment and instruction.

Instructional applications of the microcomputer are discussed by Torgesen. He explores applications with mildly handicapped children, presenting the thesis that the most promising uses will be found in programs that attempt to help these children overcome their basic skills deficits.

The area of related services is covered by Yoshida. His paper gives examples of some of the many programs and microcomputer-based devices that are helping special students to more effectively interact with their environment. In addition, he offers criteria for evaluating the cost-effectiveness of such applications.

Semmel and his colleagues explore considerations relevant to helping personnel develop the competencies needed to effectively use microcomputers in special education programs. These authors argue that the ultimate success of microcomputer applications in special education is dependent upon the extent to which teachers are computer literate and prepared to integrate these innovations into their current educational programs.

Three papers center upon concerns that can be broadly grouped under the heading of administration. Bennett presents an approach to evaluating microcomputer programs that emphasizes attention to program design, implementation, and impact. Assessing the readiness of schools for microcomputer programs is the subject of a paper by Illback and Hargan. These authors discuss a series of factors to consider in assessing school readiness and present a case study illustrating the method's utility. Finally, suggestions for managing microcomputer programs are offered by Hayden.

The effective application of microcomputer technology to special education greatly depends on the extent to which professionals understand the problems and potential benefits associated with this promising innovation. We hope this collection plays some small role in fostering such an understanding.

REFERENCE

Maher, C. A., & Bennett, R. (1984). *Planning and evaluating special education services.* Englewood Cliffs, NJ: Prentice-Hall.

Computer-Based Assessment of Special-Needs Students

Ted S. Hasselbring

ABSTRACT. The assessment of special-needs students is recognized as an important but somewhat troublesome task for many educators. Emerging microcomputer technology can be used to overcome some of the inherent problems in the assessment process. This article describes how microcomputers are currently being used in the assessment of reading and spelling skills. In addition, an overview of "expert systems" is provided, as well as a discussion of how this segment of the field of artificial intelligence is beginning to be used in the assessment of special-needs students.

Over the past few years, special educators have come to recognize the importance of assessment in the education of special-needs students. For example, the assessment of infants and young children can lead to the early identification of serious disorders that can be addressed through early intervention programs. The assessment of students as they enter school can lead to the identification of high-risk learners for whom compensatory programs can be provided. Finally, assessment for instructional planning can assist the teacher in deciding what and how to teach. Zigmond, Vallecorsa, and Silverman (1983) suggest that assessment is a necessary and integral part of teaching; it provides teachers and other personnel with the information upon which sound educational decisions can be made.

Unfortunately, the assessment of special-needs students is not without problems. As Bennett (1983) points out, those individuals responsible for carrying out the assessment process are often unqualified, the assessment tools themselves are sometimes technically inadequate, and much assessment is carried out in a biased manner. In addition, the assessment of special-needs students is a labor-in-

---

Requests for reprints should be sent to: Ted S. Hasselbring, Department of Special Education, George Peabody College for Teachers, Vanderbilt University, Nashville, Tennessee 37203.

tensive process requiring a significant amount of time and effort; most special teachers do not have the time required to regularly evaluate the progress of their students. The end result of these problems is that a large number of students are receiving services and instruction that do not fully meet their specific educational needs.

The problems associated with assessment are not easily solved. Recently, however, both regular and special educators have speculated on how microcomputer technology can be used to improve the assessment processes. For example, one of the major recommendations coming from a recent U.S. Education Department conference on the future of computers in education was that more time and effort be spent on researching how computers can be used in the assessment and diagnosis of student learning problems. In the final report of the conference, Lesgold and Reif (1983) wrote:

> Computer diagnosticians would make teachers more aware of the ways in which procedural skill and conceptual knowledge combine to produce good performance. They could show them which components are deficient in any particular student and help them become aware of areas in which all of their students need further work. (p. 20)

Computer-based assessment is currently in its infancy. Nevertheless, microcomputers are beginning to be used successfully in the assessment of special-needs students (Hasselbring & Crossland, 1982; Owens, Fox, & Hasselbring, in press). The purpose of this article is to provide some examples of how current microcomputer technology can be used to assess special-needs students. Included will be a discussion of how the microcomputer can alleviate some of the common problems associated with the assessment process. Finally, a short overview of the emerging field of "expert systems" will be presented, as well as a discussion of how this branch of artificial intelligence will likely provide the next major advancement in computer-based assessment.

COMPUTER-BASED ASSESSMENT OF SPECIAL-NEEDS CHILDREN: CURRENT DEVELOPMENTS

At present, computer-based assessment instruments generally fall into interactive or non-interactive categories. Non-interactive programs are used by an examiner for scoring, analyzing, and sometimes writing reports on commonly used standardized tests such as the WISC-R, WAIS-R, PIAT, Stanford-Binet, and the Woodcock-Johnson Psycho-Educational Battery. Using this type of program, the examiner simply enters a student's scores from the administration of the test. The computer then summarizes and prints out the results in report form. The primary advantage of this type of program is that time is saved by freeing the examiner from such clerical tasks as adding raw scores, looking through conversion tables, and in some cases, writing reports. With these programs, the assessment instrument is administered in its traditional form and the student does not interact with the computer at all.

The second type of computer-based assessment instrument currently being used with special-needs populations is interactive. Here an assessment instrument has been encoded in the form of a computer program. The computer is responsible for carrying out the complete assessment, often without the need for examiner intervention. The advantages of this type of assessment are obvious. For one, huge savings in examiner time can be accrued. This is especially important if the classroom teacher is responsible for carrying out the assessment. Also, examiner bias, administration and scoring errors, and invalid interpretations can be controlled more tightly and often eliminated.

The notion of interactive assessment can be applied to a variety of content areas. Two areas in which interactive assessment instruments have been used successfully are reading and spelling.

Reading Assessment

The assessment of reading ability in the learning handicapped student is a problem faced by most special education teachers. Of all of the discrete reading skills that diagnosticians commonly evaluate, comprehension is generally recognized to be one of the most troublesome. One reason that comprehension is difficult to assess is that much of the time learning handicapped students can successfully "word call," giving the impression that they understand what they are reading, while in reality, they understand little. To assess comprehension, teachers must either administer a standardized instrument, informally have the student read a passage of text and then ask the student questions about the passage, employ techniques such as a Cloze procedure, or use a combination of these techniques. Needless to say, this can be an extremely time consuming and tedious process. Currently, there are several microcomputer programs designed for assisting in the assessment of reading comprehension. These programs eliminate the need for one-to-one teacher administration, scoring, and analysis.

One such program is the Computerized Test of Reading Comprehension (CTORC) (Hasselbring, 1983). The CTORC is a computerized version of the widely used Test of Reading Comprehension or TORC (Brown, Hammill, & Wiederholt, 1978). The TORC is a norm-referenced test designed to assess several of the comprehension skills required in reading. The original paper and pencil version is appropriate for students in grades 2 through high school who have sufficient word recognition skills to read the test materials (at least a second grade reading level is required). Students must be able to read silently, work independently, and record their answers on a separate answer sheet.

To administer the paper and pencil version of the TORC considerable care and effort are required. For example, in most of the eight subtests, the student continues to answer questions until a ceiling of three errors out of any five consecutive items is reached. The assessor must watch the student's answer sheet closely and keep track of the most recent five responses in order to correctly implement this criterion. In addition, several subtests require that the student mark two responses to each question and credit is given only if both responses are correct. Subtest raw scores must be computed with care since different point values are given for the tasks composing different subtests.

The computerized version of the TORC removes much of the need for teacher involvement in administration, scoring, and analysis. With the computerized version, the student completes the test by interacting directly with the computer. Passages for the subtests are presented on the computer screen and questions are answered by the student on the keyboard. The student's responses are constantly monitored by the computer and when a subtest ceiling is reached the computer stores the student's responses on disk and allows the student to move to another subtest or end the session. At any point the teacher can have the computer print out a profile indicating the student's level of performance.

In a study which compared student results on the computer and written versions of the TORC, no significant differences were found between students' responses on the two forms of the test (Hasselbring, Goin, & Carruthers, 1984). Forty subjects, both handicapped and non-handicapped, were given both the written and computerized versions of the TORC using a counterbalanced design. The students performed equally well on both versions of the test. This suggests that students do not perform more poorly as a result of being tested on the computer. There *were* significant differences, however, with respect to the amount of teacher time required to administer, score, and interpret the two forms. As one would expect, the amount of teacher time required on the computerized version was significantly less than that required for the standard paper and pencil version. The results of this study suggest that the computerized version of the TORC provides the same results as the written form with a significant savings in teacher time and effort.

Another method that is often used to assess reading comprehension is the Cloze procedure (Bormuth, 1968; Jongsma, 1971). Using this technique, the student is presented with a short reading passage in which every fifth (or nth) word has been replaced with a blank. The student's task is to identify the appropriate words to insert into the blanks. From the student's responses it can be determined relatively easily whether or not the student is comprehending what is being read.

To use the Cloze procedure as an informal assessment device, the teacher must construct the assessment by typing or printing a representative passage and leaving out the target words. Then after the student has completed the passage, it must be hand scored. Much or all of this can be accomplished using the Computerized Cloze Procedure (CCP) program (Hasselbring & Kinzer, 1984). For example, using the word processing capability of the computer, text samples can be entered rapidly into the machine. These text samples can be converted into the Cloze passages using the CCP which replaces each nth word with a blank. The passage can then be printed on paper with deletions in place, accompanied by a scoring key. If the teacher elects, the CCP can present either a teacher entered text passage or a pre-programmed text passage. The program then allows the student to type the missing words in the correct spaces and scores the student's responses. The CCP provides the teacher with a fully automated Cloze procedure that allows for the assessment of comprehension while reducing the amount of time that must be invested in the assessment process.

Spelling Assessment

Probably the most effective form of spelling assessment occurs when the student writes a dictated word and this word is analyzed for errors in rules and spelling strategies. Unfortunately, this is also the most difficult type of assessment to conduct. Hence, few commercial assessment instruments contain an effective means for analyzing spelling error patterns. Those instruments which do provide an error analysis require special expertise and an inordinate amount of time to score, especially when students are experiencing severe spelling problems. For example, the Spelling Errors Test (Spache, 1981) provides an error analysis which requires hand scoring of 120 words distributed across 12 error categories. The test may take up to several hours to score for a single student.

The Computerized Test of Spelling Errors (Hasselbring, 1983) is one computer-based assessment program which represents the best concepts engendered in a number of existing standardized spelling tests. The Computerized Test of Spelling Errors (CTSE) consists of 40 words which represent three different word types, thirteen error types, and four error tendencies, thus providing the classroom teacher with a comprehensive analysis of student spelling problems. The CTSE can be administered, scored, analyzed and summarized entirely on a microcomputer.

When the student is ready to begin the test, a computer-controlled cassette recorder plays a pre-recorded tape which pronounces the target word, uses it in a sentence, and then says the word in isolation a second time. The student is prompted to type the correct spelling on the keyboard. The next word is not presented until a response is typed by the student. Thus, the speed of presentation is totally controlled by the student.

As the student types each word, the microcomputer internally scores the response and stores this information. The analysis paradigm used in the program consists of checking the student's word against the correct spelling and if correct, moving to the next word. If incorrect, the word is checked for each of the thirteen error types followed by a check for the error tendencies. If an error type or tendency is found, its occurrence is recorded and the error check resumes.

The diagnostic summary of the CTSE provides the teacher with a comprehensive breakdown of the student's performance. The summary includes a listing of the student's: (1) demographic data, (2) test summary, (3) responses, and (4) diagnostic error analysis. An example of a diagnostic summary is shown in Table 1. The demographic data simply provide the teacher with information on the student and the testing situation. The test summary and the list of student responses give general information about the student's performance. The diagnostic error analysis provides the teacher with the most useful information. Specific error types are identified as well as the student's performance on each of these error types. From the error analysis, the teacher can identify areas of strength and weakness in the spelling process and instructional prescriptions can be made.

Research using the Computerized Test of Spelling Errors and other similar computerized spelling assessments has demonstrated

TABLE 1
Computerized Test of Spelling Errors
Evaluation Summary

I. Demographic Data

Student's Name: SAKIMA   Date of Examination: 05/18/81

Birthdate: 05/14/72   Chronological Age: 9 - 0

Grade: 3   School:

Examiner: SDO   Place of Examination:

Elapsed Examination Time: 00:30:58

II. Summary

Number of Words Correct: 20   Percent of Words Correct: 50%

Number of Words Incorrect: 20   Percent of Words Incorrect: 50%

III. Listing of Student's Responses

Words Spelled Correctly	Words Spelled Incorrectly
ARROW	ANKEL (ANKLE)
ATE	FLYS (FLIES)
BULL	MILLON (MELON)
BAKE	ASELP (ASLEEP)
AWHILE	GUINT (GIANT)
BORN	LATTER (LATER)
DARK	JUMPPING (JUMPING)
HER	DURKED (DROPPED)
CUTTING	POW (PAW)
LAUGHING	FEILD (FIELD)
AM	THOW (THOUGH)
DRUM	HAMER (HAMMER)
LOOKED	CIRKER (CRACKER)
GIRL	BABYS (BABIES)
HOPED	ALOON (ALONE)
PONY	PARTYES (PARTIES)
BROOM	OBAY (OBEY)
MARCH	FATHER (FARTHER)
STREET	PEICE (PIECE)
BOXES	AME (AIM)

TABLE 1 (continued)

IV. Diagnostic Error Analysis

A. Word Types

		Number Incorrect	Percent Incorrect
1.	Regular	1 out of 6	16
2.	Predictable	12 out of 20	60
3.	Irregular	7 out of 14	50

B. Error Types

Vowels

1.	Schwa vowel sound	1 out of 5	20
2.	Short vowel sound	3 out of 10	30
3.	Long vowel sound	0 out of 11	0
4.	Digraphs and diphthongs	6 out of 11	54
5.	R-controlled vowels	1 out of 10	10

Consonants

6.	Initial position	0 out of 24	0
7.	Medial position	1 out of 23	4
8.	Final position	0 out of 12	0
9.	Blends and digraphs	4 out of 13	30

Generalizations and Patterns

10.	Suffixes	2 out of 11	18
11.	Affixation rules	4 out of 5	80
12.	Orthographic patterns	3 out of 6	50
13.	Final E rule	1 out of 5	20

C. Error Tendencies

14.	Omissions	Number of words with omissions = 8
15.	Insertions	Number of words with insertions = 3
16.	Substitutions	Number of words with substitutions = 14 Total number of letters substituted = 16
17.	Order Errors	Number of words with order errors = 5 Total number of order errors = 5

that students' responses on the microcomputer yield results similar to those obtained using a traditional paper and pencil format (Hasselbring & Crossland, 1982; Owens, Fox, & Hasselbring, in press). In two separate studies including more than sixty handicapped and non-handicapped students, error analyses from computerized and paper and pencil tests showed no significant differences between the two forms of assessment. These findings suggest that the results obtained using a computer-based spelling assessment can provide the classroom teacher with an assessment of student spelling problems that is as valid and reliable as that produced by a paper and pencil version, but without the associated tedium of personally administering and hand scoring the measure. Further, this research has shown that the microcomputer allows the student to self-pace during the assessment and that scoring errors are significantly reduced.

The results of these early attempts at interactive computer-based assessment have been quite encouraging. Through the use of computerized reading and spelling assessments, more dependable educational diagnoses can be made by teachers who in the past had neither the time nor special training required to analyze the specific learning problems of special-needs students.

EXPERT SYSTEMS: THE FUTURE OF COMPUTER-BASED ASSESSMENT?

What does the future of computer-based assessment hold? Consider for a moment a computer system that stores the knowledge, judgment, and intuition of the country's best educational diagnosticians. From this system the information can be called up at any time to assist you, step-by-step, in the assessment of your students. Programs such as this are currently being used in other fields. These programs are called *expert systems*. Expert systems have evolved from the field of artificial intelligence and can be defined as computer programs capable of reaching a level of performance comparable to that of a human expert in some specialized problem domain (Nau, 1983). Expert systems are unlike conventional application programs in that they are the first systems designed to help humans solve complex problems in a commonsense way. These systems use the methods and information acquired and developed by a human expert to solve problems, make predictions, suggest possible treatments, and offer advice that is as accurate as its human counterpart.

While expert systems in the field of education are only in the early phases of development and are not yet commercially available, corresponding systems are used commercially in other fields. The most notable expert systems are found in the field of medicine. For example, a system called MYCIN is used to assist physicians in the diagnosis of blood and meningitis infections and to recommend drug treatment. PUFF is an expert system that diagnoses pulmonary diseases by measuring lung function while ONCOCIN plans drug therapy for cancer patients. CADUCEUS, a more advanced expert system, covers the broad field of internal medicine and assists in the diagnosis of most adult illnesses.

Expert systems are designed to perform the same role as the human expert consultant, that is, provide advice in situations where highly specific knowledge and experience is needed. Ideally, an expert system should provide the user with the same information and play the same role as a human expert when placed in the same situation. For example, a medically oriented expert system might guide an inexperienced intern by asking relevant questions about the case. The intern would respond by answering these questions. The intern continues this dialog with the computer until the expert system has sufficient data on which to make a diagnosis. At this point, the intern either accepts the diagnosis or simply uses the computer's diagnosis as another piece of data since these systems are intended to complement, not replace, the physician's judgment and intuition.

Expert systems are by no means restricted to the field of medicine. Systems that emulate a human expert have been designed to assist in diesel locomotive repair, aid geologists in evaluating mineral sites, configure computer systems, diagnose plant diseases, assist oil exploration, and determine the chemical structure of complex organic molecules.

Current expert systems technology seems best suited to diagnosis or classification problems whose solutions depend primarily on the possession of a large amount of specialized, factual, and empirical knowledge (Duda & Shortliffe, 1983). Thus, it is only logical that expert systems be developed in education for assessing and diagnosing learning problems. While the reading and spelling programs discussed earlier in this article were designed to provide the teacher with some of the characteristics of an expert system, by definition, these programs are not true expert systems.

Currently, several expert systems are under development which are designed to assist in the diagnosis and assessment of learning problems. One such prototypic system developed by Colburn (1982) is designed to assist the classroom teacher in the assessment of learning disabilities. In its present form, the system is only capable of guiding the user through the stages of reading assessment. At each stage, this system analyzes the available data and suggests an appropriate next step. Depending upon the available data, the system may request information regarding the student's academic history or suggest that a particular standardized test be administered. The system could also recommend consultation with a specialist or referral to an outside agency.

Unlike the reading and spelling programs described earlier, this expert system does not test the student directly, nor does it manage the testing activities. Instead, the teacher or diagnostician performs the suggested task, such as administering a specific test, and enters the resulting information into the system. After these new data have been entered, the system analyzes this information and proposes the next step in the assessment process. Eventually, the system provides a summary of its diagnostic findings along with a prescription, including appropriate remedial strategies and instructional techniques.

With this system, a dialogue is conducted between the user and the computer with the system posing questions or making suggestions. If the desired information is not available, the system provides the diagnostician the option of stopping the dialogue in order to obtain the necessary information. In some cases where it is impossible to obtain the desired information the system is capable of handling incomplete data. However, in the case when the system must have further input in order to continue the diagnosis, the system reiterates what data are required and then terminates the session.

The performance of this expert diagnostic system was evaluated by comparing it against human diagnosticians. When subjected to a number of test cases, it was found that the expert system's diagnostic reports were consistently good. In contrast, the diagnostic reports prepared by the human experts varied dramatically in terms of style, format, readability, relevance, and accuracy.

Probably the most advanced of the current expert systems designed for diagnosing learning problems is called DEBUGGY (Burton, 1982). DEBUGGY is designed to diagnose student errors or "bugs" in simple mathematical procedures. While not designed specifically for learning handicapped students, its use with this population could prove to be invaluable. DEBUGGY is a non-interactive program where a student's answers to a set of math problems (and the problems themselves) are entered into the system. DEBUGGY compares the student's answers against a model of possible bugs and tries to diagnose any procedural problems the student may be having in math.

An interactive version of DEBUGGY, called IDEBUGGY, has the potential for allowing a much faster, better-confirmed diagnosis because the problem sequence can be tailored to the student. IDEBUGGY presents the student with problems and, using the student's answers, generates and maintains a set of possible diagnoses. After each student response, the system decides whether to give another problem or to stop and report the diagnosis. Each new problem is determined by the state of possible diagnoses up to that point. When enough evidence for one hypothesis is collected, and there are no competing hypotheses, the system provides a diagnosis (Burton, 1982).

SUMMARY

The field of computer-based assessment, while only in the early stages of development, appears to offer great promise for overcoming many of the problems currently associated with the assessment of special-needs students. When programmed appropriately, microcomputers can play the role of the assessor, with the computer and the student interacting directly. The computer can present the student with assessment items, monitor student responses, score, interpret, and summarize the student's performance. These programs, while simple in nature, appear to be successful in saving examiner time, reducing scoring errors, and providing teachers with diagnostic information beyond that which they could normally obtain.

The diagnostic and assessment programs currently available are only precursors to the more elaborate and powerful expert systems currently under development. It is conceivable that, in the next five to ten years, expert systems will be developed which contain much of the knowledge and skill of the country's best educational diagnosticians. These systems will be able to guide an assessor through the necessary steps for the assessment of any special-needs student, test the student directly where appropriate, analyze the assessment data, and prescribe appropriate instructional strategies for remediating the student's problems. While it is unlikely that the use of computers will eliminate all of the problems we face in the assessment of special-needs students, existing research suggests that we can enhance the assessment process through the continued development and the responsible use of computer-based assessment systems.

REFERENCES

Bennett, R. (1983). Research and evaluation priorities for special education assessment. *Exceptional Children, 50*(2), 110-117.

Bormuth, J. (1968). The cloze readability procedure. *Elementary English, 45,* 429-436.

Brown, V., Hammill, D., & Wiederholt, T. J. (1978). *The test of reading comprehension.* Austin, TX: Pro-Ed.

Burton, R. (1982). Diagnosing bugs in a simple procedural skill. In D. Sleeman & J. Brown (Eds.), *Intelligent tutoring systems* (pp. 157-183). New York: Academic Press.

Colburn, M. (1982). *Computer-guided diagnosis of learning disabilities: A prototype.* Unpublished master's thesis, University of Saskatchewan, Saskatoon, Sask., Canada.

Duda, R., & Shortliffe, E. (1983). Expert systems research. *Science, 220,* 261-268.

Hasselbring, T. (1983). *Computerized test of reading comprehension* [Computer program]. Nashville, TN: Expert Systems Software.

Hasselbring, T., Goin, L., & Carruthers, B. (1984). *Computer-based assessment of reading comprehension.* Unpublished manuscript, Peabody College of Vanderbilt University, Nashville, TN.

Hasselbring, T., & Crossland, C. (1982). Application of microcomputer technology to spelling assessment of learning disabled students. *Learning Disability Quarterly, 5,* 80-82.

Hasselbring, T., & Kinzer, C. (1984). *Computerized cloze procedure* [Computer program]. Nashville, TN: Expert Systems Software.

Hasselbring, T., & Owens, S. (1983). Microcomputer-based analysis of spelling errors. *Computers, Reading, and Language Arts, 1,* 26-31.

Jongsma, E. (1971). *The cloze procedure as a teaching technique.* Newark, DE: International Reading Association.

Lesgold, A., & Reif, F. (1983). *Computers in education: Realizing the potential.* Washington, DC: U.S. Government Printing Office.

Nau, D. (1983). Expert computer systems. *IEEE Computer,* (16), 63-85.

Owens, S., Fox, B., & Hasselbring, T. (in press). The microcomputer: An investigation of its effectiveness for diagnosing spelling errors. *Diagnostique.*

Spache, G. (1981). Spelling errors test. In G. Spache (Ed.), *Diagnosing and correcting reading disabilities* (2nd ed.). Boston: Allyn & Bacon.

Zigmond, N., Vallecorsa, A., & Silverman, R. (1983). *Assessment for instructional planning in special education.* Englewood Cliffs, New Jersey: Prentice-Hall, Inc.

The Microcomputer as Perceptual Tool: Searching for Systematic Learning Strategies With Handicapped Infants

Richard P. Brinker

ABSTRACT. The microcomputer as a medium of instruction is not inherently better or worse than any other medium be it lecture, television, print or practical experience. However, the microcomputer can simultaneously present instruction and collect data on student performance. In order for educators to evaluate the success of instruction presented by computer they must use the microcomputer as a perceptual tool to more sensitively monitor and modify the educational process. Thoughtful consideration of monitoring data by special educators promises to make the microcomputer a revolutionary aspect of school instruction. Such an educational revolution can extend to the delivery of special services provided that the time and ancillary supports needed to utilize performance are made available to school personnel.

Tantulus was a son of Zeus and much loved by all the gods. In response to this love, Tantalus developed a greatly exaggerated self-esteem. He scorned the gods and for this they developed a special form of punishment. The gods sent Tantalus to stand in a pool in Hades surrounded by trees hung with ripe fruit. Every time he reached for the fruit a breeze blew it just out of reach. Every time Tantalus stooped to relieve his eternal thirst the pool dried up.

American educators seem to have gotten into the same predicament as Tantalus. Whatever the cause of present concern for the educational crisis in America (National Commission on Excellence in Education, 1983), many hope that the development of microcomputer technology will provide one path out of it. However, like the fruit and the pond to which Tantalus was consigned, the microcom-

---

Requests for reprints should be sent to: Richard P. Brinker, Division of Education Policy Research and Services, Educational Testing Service, Princeton, New Jersey 08541.

© 1984 by The Haworth Press, Inc. All rights reserved.

puter has teased educators with its possibilities, but has left them with unsatisfactory solutions to their needs and the needs of their students.

In comparison to the regular educator, the special service provider faces both a wider range of possible uses for microcomputer technology as well as greater potential for misuse. Especially dramatic progress has occurred through the use of microcomputers as prosthetic devices, such as speech synthesizers, talking terminals, and optical reading machines for people with serious motor and sensory impairments. The dream that microcomputers will transform reality for handicapped people is made real when individuals who have never spoken can talk intelligibly and blind people can read books (Loebl & Kantrov, 1984; Pollard, 1984).

Alternatively, microcomputers can be used inappropriately to standardize curricula for various groups of handicapped students before the benefits of such curricula have been demonstrated (Brinker, in press). Most available special educational software uses the microcomputer as a sophisticated medium for presenting problems and providing feedback for student responses. Typically, problems found in mathematics and language arts workbooks are presented on the computer screen for the student to practice. Drill and practice exercises presented by microcomputer may become the predominant use within special education while innovative programming environments such as LOGO (Papert, 1980; Weir, 1981) are only made available to accelerated groups of students in regular education (The Computer Use Study Group, 1983). Soon we will be able to respond to that dewy commendation, "You must be very patient" by replying, "Not really, but my computer is." If there is differential application of the microcomputer as a medium for presenting traditional instruction versus as a programming environment for exploration it will be unfortunate. Handicapped students may be exposed to a curriculum which is even more dissociated from their existing skills than are current curricula (Brinker, in press). For example, use of the microcomputer to provide *only* drill and practice exercises for handicapped students could produce a greater divergence between those students already failing within the educational system, a greater divergence between rich and poor.

It is essential in the early stages of the technology revolution for special services professionals to articulate a personal philosophy regarding the purpose and use of new technologies and the anticipated benefits for various groups of students. Without such a philosophy, the application of technology to education will be dictated by marketing concerns and concerns for maximizing short-term profit while minimizing development costs. The purpose of the present paper is to provide alternative perspectives which special services professionals might adopt regarding the role of microcomputers in solving educational problems of handicapped students. First, three views of the role of microcomputers in special education are outlined. Then the evolution of an intervention program for handicapped infants and multiply handicapped preschoolers is considered from the perspective of the microcomputer as a perceptual tool. Finally, this philosophy is projected into the future where the emerging technology of "intelligent" software will be the key to providing effective services for handicapped students.

THE ROLE OF THE MICROCOMPUTER IN SPECIAL SERVICES

Microcomputers can facilitate the delivery of special services by: (1) directly teaching students; (2) reducing the amount of time taken in managing complex record systems, in retrieving data, and in generating reports; and (3) focusing the perceptions of special services personnel by enabling them to discover in handicapped students skills which had not been previously noticed. When using the microcomputer to directly teach students, the content, sequence, and feedback contingencies of an educational intervention must be precisely characterized. This use of the microcomputer for programmed instruction has a strong foundation in basic operant research and relies upon the theory that contingencies of reinforcement are the primary mechanism that shapes behavior (Skinner, 1968). The microcomputer's capacity to produce graphic, written, and auditory stimuli make it a good vehicle for providing a higher rate of feedback for student performance.

When the microcomputer is used as an information manager, one can access, review, and update information about a student and generate reports about student progress. Information management has received the most attention from software developers since the potential business market for such software is very large. Review of this role for microcomputers in education and of the microcomputer as teacher are available from other sources (Allard & Thorkildsen, 1981; Bennett, 1982; Hofmeister, 1982; White, 1984; Wilson, 1981).

Finally, the microcomputer can be employed as a perceptual tool that enables one to quickly manipulate information about a student or group of students, graphically depict such information, formulate hypotheses about past performance, and test such hypotheses through new intervention plans. This perspective—the microcomputer as perceptual tool—merges the first two perspectives with the active, problem solving role of the special services professional. Without such a merger, microcomputers will offer little progress for special services personnel, especially as they deal with more serious cognitive handicaps.

MICROCOMPUTER AS PERCEPTUAL TOOL

The unique property of microcomputers as perceptual tools derives from the capacity to store information on floppy disk which enables one to answer questions about performance by using an easily retrievable and ever-expanding data base. Empirical evidence gathered across time for a particular student can enable the special services professional to formulate intervention hypotheses. Based upon the outcome of suggested interventions, these hypotheses can be frequently re-evaluated, new interventions can be designed, and teaching can be better focussed upon the handicapped student's learning problems. How this process has worked in the course of developing an intervention program which focussed on very early learning by handicapped infants will be illustrated below (Brinker & Lewis, 1982a, 1982b). Thus, as one's understanding of the learning problems of handicapped students evolves, it is possible to return to performance data with questions which reflect this evolution. This can lead to scientific progress in the solution of educational problems of handicapped students in that new educational approaches can be empirically designed with better prediction of outcomes. Bricker (1976) has noted the utility of publicly sharing the empirical basis for promising educational techniques. However, full use of the microcomputer as a perceptual tool presumes that special services personnel are actively engaged in questioning their conclusions about handicapped students and sharing the basis for such conclusions with other special services personnel. In order for that to occur there will need to be a redefinition of the roles of many special services personnel, and reorganization of the structure of educational services to handicapped students. We will return later in this paper to consideration of such restructuring of roles to fully utilize the emerging technologies.

Applications of Microcomputers to Teaching Infants

The fundamental importance of early contingencies between infants' behavior and environmental consequences has been apparent for some time (Lewis & Goldberg, 1969; Piaget, 1952; Watson, 1966). A variety of research has led to the conclusion that handicapped infants are at high risk for learned helplessness (Seligman, 1975). Thus, in addition to other limitations, such individuals may have such limited experience exerting control over their environment that they learn not to try to affect the people and things around them (Provence & Lipton, 1962; Ramey, Sparling, & Wasik, 1981). The parents of handicapped infants have often been given bleak advice regarding the developmental potential of their children (Adams, 1982; Wolraich & Siperstein, 1983). By intervening in the infant's home it is hoped that contingencies can be arranged to provide the infant with experiences controlling environmental events while the parent witnesses the effect of such experiences. The graphics capability of microcomputers makes it possible to share an analysis of the infant's learning immediately after the instructional session. Such analysis provides parents with a new view of their infant as purposeful and competent. In addition, it provides parents with a better understanding of the nature of learning and the methods by which one might conclude that it has occurred.

The handicapped infants included in the contingency intervention project (Brinker & Lewis, 1982a,b) were selected because they showed little or no interest in the external physical world. Their parents reported that they had no favorite toys or objects. When objects were placed in their hands they dropped them instead of looking at them or putting them in their mouths. Our goal was to change these infants from this state of total lack of interest in things to a state of active search and exploration.

To provide handicapped infants with experiences controlling the environment it was necessary to detect even minimal movements by the infants. The infant was seated in an adjustable infant seat in front of a shelf on which an audio speaker, mechanical toy or rear projection screen was placed. Switches were attached to ribbons which were wrapped around the infant's wrist so that downward arm movement closed the switch and sent a signal to the microcomputer.

A carpeted panel was placed at the infant's feet so that kicking the panel sent a signal to the computer. The computer could be programmed to turn on a tape recording (e.g., with music, the mother's voice) or a variety of other mechanical devices when either kicking or downward arm movements occurred.

The goal was not to teach the infants to kick more or to wave their arms more, but rather to teach them that they could control events and more importantly, to build their motivation to control such events. The contingency intervention project success stories were those handicapped infants who actively tried to produce these consequences by systematically changing their behavior when the contingencies were changed. Such changes generally included not only increases in the rate of movements which were being reinforced but also increases in smiling and vocalizing. Although the goals of the contingency intervention were more limited than those found in the typical intervention program, the motivation to explore and control the environment is a fundamental component underlying performance in a variety of areas, a process closely related to the infant's general development in the first year of life (Yarrow et al., 1983).

In 1979 when we first bought an Apple II microcomputer, our assumptions about the ease of using such a device were naive. We hoped that the microcomputer could be left in the home so that parents could load the appropriate diskette containing their infant's program of contingencies. Then the parents could sit back and watch their handicapped baby actively engage in turning on various consequences and at the same time view a learning curve on the family TV as it inched its way to a pre-set criterion. Two problems with these assumptions were that (1) the level of computer literacy in American homes was not sufficiently advanced so that parents could be easily taught to use the microcomputer for these purposes and (2) the belief that infants, especially handicapped infants, are capable of learning to control such environmental events was not common knowledge. Our assumptions of five years ago are becoming progressively more appropriate as microcomputers are marketed to an increasing number of American homes and as the national media such as Time, Newsweek, and Reader's Digest feature articles on the previously unnoticed abilities of infants. Today the research on infant learning provides convincing evidence of the importance of the co-occurrences between infant behavior and environmental consequences for subsequent psychological development of handicapped infants (Brinker & Lewis, 1982a; Watson, Hayes & Vietze, 1982).

It was surprising to find some handicapped infants actively exploring the situation within a few minutes exposure to a contingency (Brinker & Lewis, 1981). These infants seem to have come into the situation with a behavioral hypothesis which when confirmed by the contingency produced clear diffcrentiation of reinforced from nonreinforced responses. Other infants learned in an incremental fashion, gradually differentiating reinforced from nonreinforced responses over a period of days or weeks. The microcomputer graphics showed these different patterns of learning immediately after the contingency intervention sessions. These same graphics programs made it possible to share this discovery with the infant's parents and to involve them in planning the next contingency.

Thus, the Apple II did make it possible to bring complex laboratory control routines from the operant conditioning laboratory into the home. However, the technology was foreign to most parents and teachers. The flexibility offered by the contingency intervention system for adjusting response requirements and consequences to the individual child was obtained at the cost of specialized knowledge. It took careful preparation to set up contingencies so infants' movements were properly recorded by the computer and the right consequences were provided to the infant at the right time. Learning to detect what error prevented the system from operating required specialized skills. The idea of placing the computer with a preplanned program in the home so that parents might implement it was not viable. Once everything was appropriately connected and the correct program was tested and loaded, the computer could do the teaching in the sense of controlling contingencies. However, the infants only learned if the contingency provided novel consequences for behavior under their control. Once they had shown a differential increase in reinforced behavior over other forms of behavior, handicapped infants demanded changes in the contingencies with which they were confronted.

Thus, a more basic problem extending beyond simple implementation of contingencies was actively monitoring the performance in the most recent session relative to the history of the infant's performance. This monitoring became critical in each session because even very young handicapped infants required sensitive modification of contingencies in order to maintain their interest. For example, after a few days during which the infants experienced 14 minutes of contingency between arm movement and the production of a musical consequence, they would tire of that arrangement. Sessions had to be stopped halfway through because of fretting and crying by the infant. When a new contingency was introduced in the subsequent session the infant invariably showed renewed interest and sustained performance for a full 14 minutes. Note that 14 minutes of sustained interest and activity without adult mediation is a relatively long time for infants in the first year of life.

A constant challenge was to change contingencies frequently enough so that the infant learned without developing an aversion to the learning situation. Ultimately, simple decision rules were built into the software so that the microcomputer could change contingencies based upon ongoing analysis of the infant's behavior. When signs of satiation were detected through decrements in response rate relative to the rate in previous sessions, the microcomputer changed the consequence, the schedule of reinforcement, or the effective response. On several occasions such within-session changes produced dramatic changes in the infant's emotional state. The new learning problem reduced the crying and fretting and the infant increased the rate of responding. The implication of such phenomena is that the special service provider is *not* called upon to be patient. Rather he or she must be actively engaged in providing new learning problems to the handicapped child which are presented immediately upon solution of preceding problems and which are an optimal challenge to the child. Hunt (1961) has emphasized that the optimal challenge is a problem which demands a recombination of existing skills.

Using the Perceptual Tool. The microcomputer made it possible not only to present handicapped infants with contingencies of reinforcement, but also automatically stored a record of that performance which could be immediately depicted as a graph. This graph informs a perceiver—the special service provider and parents—who can use the microcomputer as a tool with which to make decisions. Perception requires some framework within which information is interpreted and made more meaningful. Many of the parents and some of the teachers with whom we have worked did not have such a framework for perceiving the learning of handicapped infants. They often have made the simple mistake of equating the arrangement of contingencies with learning by the child. This fallacy has its roots in the novelty for most adults of seeing infants or severely handicapped children turn on slide projectors, tape recorders, or battery operated toys. Although the mechanism by which the infant produces such results is initially accidental—simply a function of environmental engineering—it is nevertheless startling to an onlooker and seems something of an accomplishment for the infant when such consequences occur. Nevertheless, the question of importance is whether the infant has *intentionally* emitted the behavior to produce the consequence.

This question of learning demands a relative view of the infant's behavior, a view which requires a comparison of the rate and quality of the behavior under different conditions. Thus, to document learning requires considerable effort on the part of special services personnel which goes beyond the design of the contingencies in the learning situation. Moreover, without such documentation it is not possible to modify contingencies in such a way that simple behaviors which have been learned become elaborated into more complex and general behavioral strategies. While the microcomputer can be used to facilitate the implementation of contingencies to promote learning, it will not substitute for the special services professional's time in documenting that learning has occurred, in determining the next step for a handicapped child, or in deciding when to take it.

The contingency intervention project used two comparison conditions from which learning could be inferred. The first comparison condition was a 3 minute baseline during which the rate of the behavior to be learned was recorded in the absence of any consequent events. The second comparison was between the rate of reinforced behavior and the rates of behaviors which were not reinforced through programmed consequences. This second comparison is commonly called a multiple baseline (Sidman, 1960). During intervention sessions, a consequence was programmed to occur either for arm movements or for foot movements. These two types of baselines provided the basis for making two sorts of conclusions about the infant's learning. Specifically, the baseline was used to document a basic contingency awareness while the multiple baseline was used to distinguish intentional behavior to produce consequences from behavior which resulted from general arousal.

If the rate of behavior is consistently higher during contingent reinforcement than it was during the initial baseline, then it can be concluded that the infant has learned a general expectation that his activity controlled environmental events (Lewis & Goldberg, 1969). From the infant's point of view there is a basic awareness that "I can make things happen" (Watson, 1966). Such knowledge may simply be a function of the infant's neurological and muscular system such that the consequence produces general arousal of which the reinforced response is a part. Thus, the infant with simple contingency awareness doesn't necessarily know how he makes things happen. For example, in Figure 1A both the rate of pulling (A) and the rate of kicking (L) increase although only kicking is actually programmed to produce a consequence.

The second type of comparison, a multiple baseline, provides the basis for determining whether the infant is intentionally varying behavior to reproduce the consequence. This pattern of behavior includes an increase in rate of the reinforced response and a simultaneous *decrease* in the rate of a nonreinforced response (see Figure 1B). Down's syndrome infants as young as 3 months of age have shown such a pattern of learning. Moreover this pattern has been replicated when new contingencies were arranged so previously *ineffective* behavior was reinforced while previously *effective* behavior no longer produced consequences (Brinker & Lewis, 1982b). This latter pattern indicates that infants not only know that they control things, but that they also know how to control things, although their options are still limited by motor immaturity.

This framework, comparison of behavior to a baseline and comparison of reinforced behavior to nonreinforced behavior, was the basis for deciding that an infant had learned and for deciding about the nature of that learning. For microcomputers to be perceptual tools, such frameworks must be developed in all the content areas which are taught to handicapped students. Although the microcomputer can be used as an intelligent interface, which makes decisions based on an ongoing analysis of the child's behavior, the problem remains: Who will write these decision rules and upon what knowledge will such rules be based? Because so little of the research on infant learning has included multiple sessions of exposure to reinforcement contingencies, it is difficult to establish the foundation for such decisions. Nevertheless, if such ongoing revision of the learning problem is required in the context of the very simple repertoires of 3-month old handicapped infants, then such sensitive revision is even more critical to foster a motivation for learning in the older handicapped child.

Data Based Decision Rules

The use of the microcomputer as a perceptual tool for "watching" the learning process and making decisions based upon data makes several presumptions about the structure of special services. First, it assumes that the same special service providers who obtain

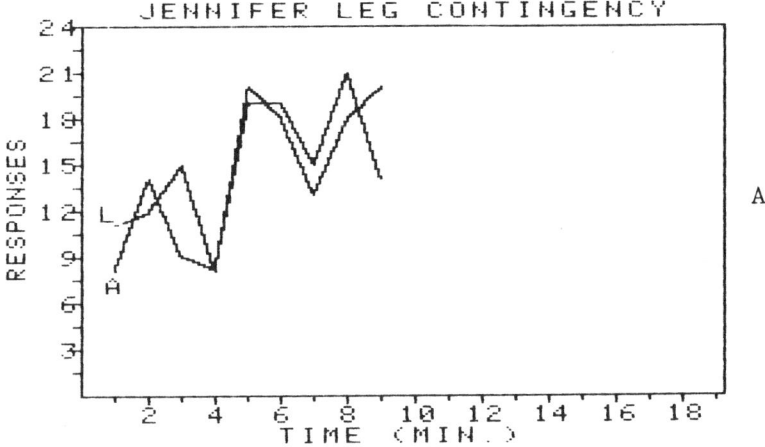

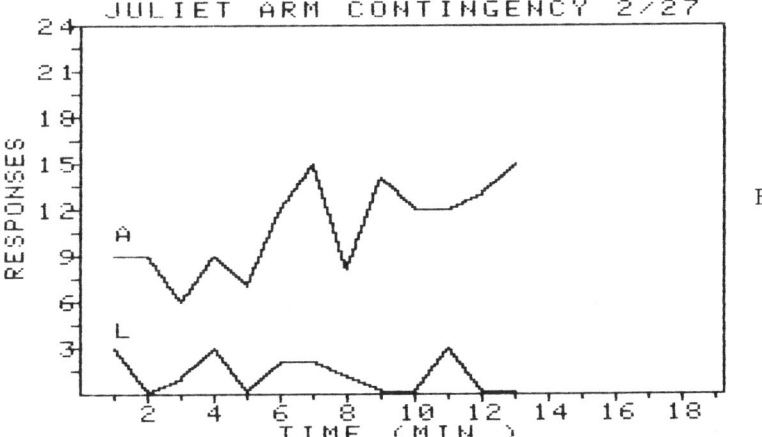

FIGURE 1. Patterns of learning by Down's Syndrome infants. (A = arm pulling; L = leg kicking.)

objective, quantifiable data about students also make educational decisions about those students' programs. Second, it assumes that the objective quantifiable data which have been obtained are pertinent to the instruction which students receive. Finally, it assumes that the data clearly imply some decision regarding a program change which is preferred over other program changes. There are some problems with making each of these assumptions, and to that extent one cannot use the microcomputer as a perceptual tool without bringing additional knowledge to the decision making process. If the full potential of microcomputers is to be made available to special service providers, then serious discussion about the organization of education for such purposes should begin.

Haring, Liberty, and White (1980) have reviewed the findings of two major projects investigating educational decision rules in programs for handicapped students. They argue that different kinds of decision rules apply at different stages of the learning process. The phases within a learning hierarchy include acquisition, fluency building, maintenance, generalization, and adaptation. Data support the notion that antecedent manipulations such as physical prompting, demonstration, and enhancement of cue salience are more effective in the acquisition phase of learning but produce little improvement during fluency building or maintenance stages of learning (Filler & Bricker, 1976; Haring et al., 1980). Strategies such as changing the consequence or schedule of reinforcement result in more improvement of performance during fluency building and generalization phases. Generalization is facilitated when different people teach the student and provide a stable set of contingencies, when the setting for training is systematically varied, and when the stimulus parameters are systematically varied within the boundaries of conceptual classes (Stokes & Baer, 1977). Very little data are available on the adaptation of learned strategies to new situations. Although this promises to be an important new direction which will influence educational intervention as part of a more general cognitive learning theory, the techniques for teaching "strategies" are only beginning to emerge (Borkowski & Cavanaugh, 1979; Brown, Campione, & Barclay, 1979; Meichenbaum & Asarnow, 1979). There is no empirical basis for deciding how to teach cognitive strategies to handicapped populations or how to change such interventions based on educational data.

The microcomputer can facilitate the development of the knowledge upon which educational decision making can be based. Initially, such knowledge will be in the form of behavioral phenomena which cause the special service provider to speculate about underlying learning processes. This phase, as in the contingency intervention project, leads to a second phase of data integration and hypothesis testing with new students. The microcomputer's capacity to be linked into local, regional, and national communication networks makes it possible to expand the number of special service providers involved in such hypothesis generation and testing. Such networks are a technologically more advanced expression of the process of publicly articulating alternative explanations and devising critical tests to eliminate some of the alternatives (Bricker, 1976). Ultimately the microcomputer can be used as an intelligent interface which models the analysis that experts in various special services would use when planning educational programs and deciding to change programs.

ARTIFICIAL INTELLIGENCE AND EXPERT SYSTEMS

Artificial intelligence research has progressed from teaching computers to play chess to modelling basic human processes such as speech recognition, language production, and problem solving (Dehn & Schank, 1982). The current artificial intelligence research seeks ways in which a computer can be programmed to quickly delimit a problem to a few possible solutions rather than to systematically search through all the possible solutions. Thus, rules are developed for restricting the possibilities to a relatively small number of solutions relative to all the possible combinations. These developments in artificial intelligence have paralleled the findings of research which compare the performance of human experts to novices (Chi, Feltovich, & Glaser, 1981). Both types of research have found that experts and "intelligent" programs recognize a broad pattern in the information given and proceed to a much smaller set of solutions than the novice or the program which systematically tests all the possible solutions. Both the expert and the "intelligent" program accomplish the early pruning of alternatives by combining a very broad knowledge base with an efficient heuristic strategy for simplifying that space.

The principles which have emerged from cognitive science and artificial intelligence research have been applied to real world problems through computer software called expert systems. Expert systems have been developed which diagnose pulmonary and blood diseases, discover mineral deposits, diagnose the source of electrical malfunctions in locomotives, determine the molecular structure of chemicals, and design customized computer systems (Hayes-Roth, Waterman, & Lenat, 1983). The next generation of microcomputers will incorporate expert systems concepts in the architecture of both the hardware and software (Feigenbaum & McCorduck, 1983).

When such concepts are built into the next generation of microcomputers it will become feasible for the program not only to control the learning situation, generate permanent performance records and analyze those records as the contingency intervention software enabled us to. In addition, decision rules such as those discussed by Haring et al. (1980) can provide advice regarding possible changes in the educational program. Moreover such advice can be based, not only upon expert opinion, but also upon an empirical analysis of the improvements associated with various types of program changes at various phases of the learning process.

When expert systems are developed to address the educational problems of handicapped students, the microcomputer will become an indispensable tool for special services professionals. Like any tool, the microcomputer will help those who are most skilled in using it. If special service providers begin now to demand the kind of microcomputer systems and programs which help them make teaching decisions then such products will become available (Colbourn, 1982). On the other hand, if we accept that the role of microcomputers is to relieve us of the tedium of providing drill and practice to handicapped learners, we will be disappointed. Once the novelty wears off, there is every reason to believe that the use of microcomputers as a medium of instruction will go the way of other such media. It is the instructional content and method, not the media, which has been shown to account for past educational impact (Clark, 1983).

Like Tantalus, we may feel that false hopes have been engendered. Special service providers have been encouraged to use the microcomputer as perceptual tool, a role which preserves the educational process and educational decision making as professional responsibilities. The microcomputer provides an information source which can be used to enhance both the quality of the educational process and the empirical basis for decision making. Expertise may be progressively built into the microcomputer software to provide educators with increasingly strong foundations for the decisions they make. Such a scenario can be accomplished in a context in which special service providers have articulated their own personal philosophy of the role of microcomputers in their work. Then educators will be able to incorporate technological innovations to discover in handicapped students skills which are keys to their learning.

REFERENCES

Adams, G. L. (1982). Referral advice given by physicians. *Mental Retardation, 20*(1), 16-20.

Allard, K., & Thorkildsen, R. (1981). Intelligent videodiscs for special education. *Videodisc News, 2*(4), 6-7.

Bennett, R. E. (1982). Applications of microcomputer technology to special education. *Exceptional Children, 49*(2), 106-113.

Borkowski, J. G., & Cavanaugh, J. C. (1979). Maintenance and generalization of skills and strategies by the retarded. In N. R. Ellis (Ed.), *Handbook of mental deficiency, psychological theory and research, Second Edition.* Hillsdale, NJ: Lawrence Erlbaum.

Bricker, W. A. (1976). Service of research. In N. G. Haring, R. D. Sherr, & L. Brown (Eds.), *Hey, don't forget about me!* Reston, VA: Council for Exceptional Children.

Brinker, R. P. (in press). Curricula without recipes: A challenge to teachers and a promise to severely retarded students. In D. Bricker & J. Filler (Eds.), *Serving the severely retarded: From research to practice.* Reston, VA: Council for Exceptional Children.

Brinker, R. P., & Lewis, M. (1981). *Patterns of learning by handicapped infants.* Paper presented at the Biennial Convention of the Society for Research in Child Development, Boston.

Brinker, R. P., & Lewis, M. (1982a). Discovering the competent handicapped infant: A process approach to assessment and intervention. *Topics in Early Childhood Education, 2*(2), 1-16.

Brinker, R. P., & Lewis, M. (1982b). Making the world work with microcomputers: A learning prosthesis for handicapped infants. *Exceptional Children, 49*(2), 163-170.

Brown, A. L., Campione, J. C., & Barclay, C. R. (1979). Training self checking routines for estimating text readiness: Generalization from list learning to prose recall. *Child Development, 50,* 501-512.

Chi, M. T., Feltovich, P. J., & Glaser, R. (1981). Categorization and representation of physics problems by experts and novices. *Cognitive Science, 5,* 121-132.

Clark, R. E. (1983). Reconsidering research on learning from media. *Review of Educational Research, 53*(4), 445-459.

Colbourn, M. J. (1982). *Computer-guided diagnosis of learning disabilities.* Master's of Education thesis submitted to the Department for the Education of Exceptional Children, University of Saskatchewan, Saskatoon, Canada. (ERIC Document Reproduction Service No. ED 222032).

Computer Use Study Group. (1983). Computers in schools: Stratifier or equalizer. *Quarterly Newsletter of the Laboratory of Comparative Human Cognition, 5*(3), 51-55.

Dehn, N., & Schank, R. (1982). Artificial and human intelligence. In R. Sternberg (Ed.), *Handbook of human intelligence.* New Rochelle, NY: Cambridge University Press.

Feigenbaum, E. A., & McCorduck, P. (1983). *The fifth generation: Japan's computer challenge to the world.* Reading, MA: Addison-Wesley.

Filler, J. W., & Bricker, W. A. (1976). Teaching styles of mothers and the match-to-sample performance of their retarded preschool-age children. *American Journal of Mental Deficiency, 80,* 504-511.

Haring, N. G., Liberty, K. A., & White, O. R. (1980). Rules for data-based strategy decisions in instructional programs: Current research and instructional implications. In W. Sailor, B. Wilcox, & L. Brown (Eds.), *Methods of instruction for severely handicapped students.* Baltimore, MD: Paul H. Brookes.

Hofmeister, A. (1982). Microcomputers in perspective. *Exceptional Children, 49*(2), 115-121.

Hunt, J. McV. (1961). *Intelligence and experience.* New York: Ronald Press.

Lewis, M., & Goldberg, S. (1969). Perceptual-cognitive development in infancy: A generalized expectancy model as a function of the mother-infant interaction. *Merrill-Palmer Quarterly, 15,* 81-100.

Loebl, D., & Kantrov, I. (1984, February). Micros in the special ed classroom. *Electronic Learning,* 38-39.

Meichenbaum, D., & Asarnow, J. (1979). Cognitive-behavior modification and metacognitive development: Implications for the classroom. In P. C. Kendall & L. D. Hollon (Eds.), *Cognitive behavioral interventions: Theory, research, and procedures* (pp. 11-35). New York: Academic Press.

National Commission on Excellence in Education. (1983). *A nation at risk: The imperative for educational reform.* Washington, DC: U.S. Government Printing Office.

Papert, S. (1980). *Mindstorms.* New York: Basic Books.

Piaget, J. (1952). *The origins of intelligence in children.* New York: International University Press.

Pollard, J. P. (1984, February). Adaptive devices for special education. *Electronic Learning,* 44-46.

Provence, S., & Lipton, R. C. (1962). *Infants in institutions.* New York: International University Press.

Ramey, C. T., Sparling, J. J., & Wasik, B. H. (1981). Creating social environments to facilitate language development. In R. L. Schiefelbusch & D. D. Bricker (Eds.), *Early language: Acquisition and intervention* (pp. 448-476). Baltimore: University Park Press.

Seligman, M. (1975). *Helplessness: On depression development and death.* San Francisco: W. H. Freeman.

Sidman, M. (1960). *Tactics of scientific research.* New York: Basic Books.

Skinner, B. F. (1968). *The technology of teaching.* New York: Appleton-Century-Crofts.

Stokes, J., & Baer, D. (1977). An implicit technology of generalization. *Journal of Applied Behavior Analysis, 10,* 349-367.

Watson, J. S. (1966). The development and generalization of contingency awareness in early infancy: Some hypotheses. *Merrill-Palmer Quarterly, 12,* 123-135.

Watson, J. S., Hayes, L. A., & Vietze, P. (1982). Response-contingent stimulation as a treatment for developmental failure in infancy. *Journal of Applied Developmental Psychology, 3*(3), 191-203.

Weir, S. (1981). Logo and the exceptional child. *Microcomputing,* 76-84.

White, G. T. (1984, February). Micros for the special ed administrator. *Electronic Learning,* 39-42.

Wilson, K. (1981). *Computers for special education management: Progress, potential, and pitfalls.* Reston, VA: ERIC Clearinghouse on Handicapped and Gifted Children.

Wolraich, M. L., & Siperstein, G. N. (1983). Assessing professionals' prognostic impressions of mental retardation. *Mental Retardation, 21*(1), 8-12.

Yarrow, L. J., McQuiston, S., McTurk, R. H., McCarthy, M. E., Klein, R. P., & Vietze, P. M. (1983). Assessment of mastery motivation during the first year of life: Contemporaneous and cross-age relationships. *Developmental Psychology, 19*(2), 159-171.

Instructional Uses of Microcomputers With Elementary Aged Mildly Handicapped Children

Joseph K. Torgesen

ABSTRACT. The goal of this article is to evaluate what we know about the instructional use of computers with young children and to suggest some priorities for their use with mildly handicapped children. While it is clear that computers can be programmed to provide effective instruction in a variety of skills, with mildly handicapped children they appear particularly suited to the delivery of highly motivational, speed oriented practice on basic academic skills in reading and math. Examples of currently available software are presented and evaluated in light of this priority, and needs for the future in terms of teacher training, service delivery systems, and hardware and software developments are discussed.

Statements that new microcomputer technology represents an enormous potential resource for educators are becoming passé. In an amazingly brief time period, educational applications of computer technology have become one of the most frequently discussed topics in education journals and meetings. Both state and national level conferences on educational computing are being sponsored at a prolific rate, and the International Association of Children and Adults with Learning Disabilities has adopted computer technology as one of the major themes for its 1984 meetings. There can be little doubt that advances in basic hardware and software technology, as well as dramatic cost reductions in both areas, are making computer resources available to educators to an extent never before possible. Although the prospect of wide use of this new and powerful technology is exciting, it also presents educators with a serious dilem-

---

Requests for reprints should be sent to: Joseph Torgesen, Department of Psychology, Florida State University, Tallahassee, Florida 32306.

© 1984 by The Haworth Press, Inc. All rights reserved.

ma. The basic problem is how to focus this technology where it will do the most good while minimizing unrealistic expectations and misuses that can only lead to frustration and disillusionment with computers as simply another educational fad.

The purpose of this article is to evaluate what we know about the instructional uses of computers with young children and to suggest some priorities for their use with mildly handicapped children. Mildly handicapped children include those labeled educably mentally retarded, learning disabled, emotionally impaired, and culturally different. These children are grouped together because it is clear that they have many of the same educational needs that can be addressed using roughly similar techniques (Hallahan & Kauffman, 1976). The discussion will focus on elementary aged children in these categories because I believe that the uses of computers with mildly handicapped adolescents will almost certainly be different from those with younger children. While the education of younger children should be focused primarily on the acquisition of academic tool skills (reading, math, spelling), the education of adolescents must necessarily focus on a variety of content areas and acquisition of more advanced study and work related skills (Deshler, Schumaker, & Lenz, in press; Deshler, Schumaker, Lenz, & Ellis, in press).

EFFECTIVENESS OF COMPUTER ASSISTED INSTRUCTION WITH YOUNG CHILDREN

What do we know for certain about the effectiveness of computer assisted instruction with elementary aged children? From one point of view, we know a great deal, while from another, we know almost nothing. The basic problem lies in the fact that there can be no general answer to questions about the effectiveness of Computer Assisted Instruction (CAI). The answer to this question depends on the specific hardware and software that is used, as well as the overall educational context in which CAI is applied. Perhaps a better question to consider is simply whether or not it is possible to program a computer to effectively aid children in the acquisition of basic skills in reading and math. If phrased this way, the answer is unequivocally affirmative.

Although the widespread use of microcomputers in schools has occurred only recently, the history of CAI with young children extends back at least 20 years (Suppes, Jerman, & Brian, 1968). Early programs using large main frame computers and employing elaborate software reported generally favorable results for instructional programs in both math (Suppes & Morningstar, 1969) and reading (Fletcher & Atkinson, 1972). Since that time, very large scale evaluations of similar software and hardware systems have confirmed the initially positive results for both reading and math in the primary grades (Hallworth & Brebner, 1980; Holland, 1980). Based on these large scale evaluations, as well as several reviews of smaller studies (Dence, 1980; Edwards, Norton, Taylor, Weiss, & Van Dusseldorf, 1975; Jamison, Suppes, & Wells, 1974; Roblyer & King, 1983), we can conclude that: (1) when used to provide practice in basic skills as an adjunct to regular instruction, as little as ten minutes a day of CAI can have a significant effect on achievement; (2) it appears easier to deliver effective CAI in math than in reading. Since both the large evaluation studies cited and many of the smaller ones used economically disadvantaged or culturally different children as subjects, there is good evidence that CAI can be a useful educational tool with children who often have difficulty learning in the regular classroom.

Although the point was made earlier, I want to emphasize that these findings are tied to the specific instructional context in which they were obtained. Almost all of the evidence about CAI effectiveness was obtained using a curriculum delivered by computers larger than the micros currently being used in schools. These computers have both advantages and disadvantages when compared to smaller computers. Most of the CAI was delivered in specially constructed computer labs, as opposed to individual classrooms or resource rooms. Finally, the curriculum itself was both more elaborate and, in some ways, more restricted, than that being offered for use on the micro-systems. Thus, although we know that some CAI configurations can be successful, we know very little about the effectiveness of most of the systems that are beginning to be widely used today.

Of course, the absence of formal evaluation results for microcomputer systems will not, and should not, deter educators from beginning to use them. Assuming that they are used in a way that is consistent with sound educational practice, children should benefit from instruction delivered by these newer systems. After all, good CAI systems simply follow many of the procedures that good teachers follow. Computers can have a positive effect on the time children spend on academic tasks; they can be programmed for mastery-based learning; they employ direct instruction and practice; the instruction they deliver can be individualized; and they can offer timely and informative feedback. All of these instructional procedures have been shown to lead to higher achievement in the regular classroom, and they are also part of most recommendations for the education of mildly handicapped children (Hammill & Bartel, 1975; Maxwell, 1980).

REMAINING QUESTIONS

Although we would expect careful application of CAI with microcomputers to be successful, there are many important questions that must be addressed as we search for the best ways to use them. For example, since computers are relatively expensive, decisions about how to use them must be considered in light of their cost effectiveness. Although early CAI using main frame or mini-computers was relatively expensive (roughly $2.00 per hour), the cost of instruction with microcomputers is much less (roughly 25-35 cents per hour). In addition, the initial investment in a beginning system is much less with micro-systems than with the larger computers. However, there are a number of low cost teaching aids/machines available, and we really have no data comparing their effectiveness with that of computers. One recent study showed that practice on basic computational skills obtained from workbooks was just as effective as that derived from a fairly elaborate drill and practice program administered on a computer (Foster & Torgesen, 1983). The computer program did have an advantage, however, in that it required less teacher time to administer than the workbook practice.

Another interesting question is whether or not future research will replicate early findings that CAI is particularly beneficial to low achieving students (Fletcher & Atkinson, 1972; Jamison, Fletcher, Suppes, & Atkinson, 1975; Tait, Hartley, & Anderson, 1974). Such a finding, of course, is especially encouraging to those interested in the education of the mildly handicapped. However, this finding has been reported only in post hoc analyses of data, and is yet to be subjected to an a priori experimental test. A final question for the future involves the relationship between teachers and computers in the classroom. Most studies have shown that CAI works effectively as a supplement to instruction by teachers. It seems likely that some subjects might be entirely taught by computers, while others must be first taught by teachers and then practiced on the computer. If teachers come to depend too heavily or inappropriately on computers to teach their students, and reduce their own level of effort accordingly, the total effect of using computers might be negative rather than positive.

PRIORITIES FOR USE OF COMPUTERS

Given the small amount of data and experience that is available to guide our use of computers in the classroom, there is a fairly broad range of opinion about how computers might best be used. Fletcher and Suppes (1972) have suggested that, "In designing computer assisted instruction, the issue is not what teachers can do and what computers can do. The problem is to allocate to teachers and computers, those tasks that each does best" (p. 45). With a tool as flexible as computers, a whole range of potential uses suggest themselves. Microcomputers have obvious motivational value (Lepper, 1982), and their graphics capabilities might be used to illustrate mathematical or scientific principles that are very difficult to communicate by other media. A variety of games and exciting learning activities might be used to build the self-confidence or change the attitudes of mildly handicapped children (Schiffman, Tobin, & Buchanan, 1982). Alternatively, computers might be used to provide experience that would build general learning or problem solving skills, since mildly handicapped children are generally deficient in the use of organized learning strategies in school (Campione & Brown, 1978; Torgesen & Licht, 1983). Finally, several authors (Lesgold, 1983; Torgesen & Young, 1983; Wilkenson, 1983) have suggested that computers can be used to provide the extensive practice that mildly handicapped children require for the attainment of rapid and efficiently executed component skills on complex tasks like reading and math. I believe that this last possibility may prove to be the most important use of microcomputers with young mildly handicapped children because it addresses a critical educational need and draws upon one of the most established strengths of CAI.

Most children with mild handicaps are deficient in basic reading and math skills, and their deficits constitute a major obstacle to overall successful adjustment in school. Certainly one of the most important reasons these children do poorly in reading and math is their failure to master the basic component processes required to understand text and solve complex math problems. Stanovich (1982) has shown that a major source of reading difficulty in young children is failure to acquire rapid and accurate word identification skills. Most poor readers cannot decode individual words as easily as good readers. Similarly, Resnick (1981) has shown that ability to function effectively in solving complex math problems depends crucially on the ability to do simple computations rapidly and accurately.

Although mildly handicapped children have a particular need for highly structured and closely monitored practice in order to master the processing operations required by academic tasks, teachers find it very difficult to provide opportunities for this kind of practice. Berliner and Rosenshine (1977) have shown that the time children spend practicing basic reading skills is quite variable from classroom to classroom, and overall is very low. Teachers also find it difficult to closely monitor both speed and accuracy of response (both of these measurements are necessary to determine if a child has mastered a component process). Children generally move from level to level in reading programs based on the accuracy of their responses with little regard to how easy it was for them to respond, or how fast they could respond (Lesgold & Resnick, 1982).

In contrast to teachers, computers are uniquely suited to delivering large amounts of closely monitored and individualized practice in basic skills. They can be programmed to provide practice in a variety of interesting formats that will maintain interest and motivation, and they have the capacity to monitor both speed and accuracy of students' responses. Thus, using computers to provide large amounts of closely monitored practice would be one way to utilize the unique capabilities of computers in the education of mildly handicapped children.

This discussion implies that computers should be used primarily in a supplemental instructional role to provide practice on skills that are first introduced and taught by teachers. At least in the area of beginning reading instruction, this was the conclusion reached by the early developers of CAI (Fletcher, 1979). Early experiments suggested that it was very difficult to anticipate the broad variety of corrective feedback that young children require in learning to read. In terms of overall cost-effectiveness, use of computers to reinforce instruction provided by teachers appeared to be the best alternative. Lesgold (1983) has also suggested that we know much more about the precise elements required for effective practice than we do about the exact ways to deliver good initial instruction. This makes it likely that we will be able to do a better job programming practice activities than developing complex tutorials for new concepts. Finally, the memory capabilities of microcomputers typically found in schools cannot support the rapid and complex branching activities of good tutorial programs, while they are completely adequate to support effective practice activities. Although personal computers are available now that do have sufficient memory to run complex branching programs, their cost is still prohibitive to schools. These machine and software limitations, coupled with the difficulties involved in providing good skill building activities by traditional means, suggest that, for the present, the most effective way to use computers with mildly handicapped children may be to increase their opportunities for practice on the component skills of academic tasks.

PROGRAMS CURRENTLY AVAILABLE IN READING AND MATH

Most current discussions of microcomputer CAI focus on limitations in the software rather than hardware. A problem until recently has been caused by lack of cooperation between educators and programmers in producing attractive and meaningful instructional programs. Programs produced by sophisticated programmers have lacked sound pedagogical design, while those produced by educators have been crude in terms of programming. Although this situation has changed dramatically in the past year, none of the software in reading and mathematics for use with microcomputers approaches the sophistication or completeness of the programs that are available for larger computers. Many of these latter programs, which have produced positive results in formal evaluations, are organized in "strands" which provide skill development in important areas of reading and math. For example, one of the programs developed at Stanford University for early reading instruction has strands covering letter identification, sight words, spelling patterns, phonics, comprehension and word vocabulary, and comprehension of sentences (Fletcher & Atkinson, 1972). This program has a complex system for keeping track of student responses in order to provide practice that is responsive to individual needs. The program also has an audio component that allows rapid (32 milliseconds) access to over 6,000 words and phrases. Both the record keeping and audio components of this program are made possible by the large memory of the computer system that supports it. The only program for micros that approaches the completeness of this software is the *Micro-Read* program published by American Educational Computer, Inc. This program employs excellent graphics and high quality audio output from digitally recorded speech to provide practice in reading ranging from phonics exercises to paragraph comprehension. Although it is a visually more attractive program than the earlier curriculum developed for larger computers, it lacks the latter program's sophisticated record keeping capabilities and also has only a limited set of practice activities in each strand. Limitations in the number of practice exercises that have an audio component are the result of the large storage requirements for digitally recorded speech. The micro-systems typically found in schools simply do not have the space available to store large quantities of digitally recorded speech. A further limitation of the *Micro-Read* program is that it does not push children to a mastery criterion in both speed and accuracy of response, but simply measures accuracy. Hopefully, programs such as *Micro-Read* can be further developed to provide both more individualized practice with larger numbers of exercises and an emphasis on speed and accuracy in the execution of component skills in reading.

Another promising program in the area of reading is the *Compensatory Reading Program* which is based on the *Processing Power* program offered by Instructional/Communications Technology, Inc. This program is much more narrow in focus than the *Micro-Read* program, but it does focus on building rapid word-reading skills. The basic rationale for the program is derived from studies of eye-movement patterns in poor readers. Children receive repeated practice reading stories presented in different visual formats. The first time they read a story all the words are presented one at a time in the same location. In successive re-readings of the story, more and more words are presented together on the screen. The program is interesting because of its elaborate theoretical rationale, and its emphasis on increasing fluency of component processes in reading. However, it employs a primitive record keeping system and requires a teacher or aid to be present while the children perform the exercises. Thus, it does not provide the kind of independent practice in reading that makes CAI such an attractive classroom tool. In addition, the program focuses on a very narrow range of instructional objectives.

Although a wider variety of programs are available for CAI in math than in reading, these programs have many of the same limitations as those in reading. One of the most complete programs, authored by Courses for Computers, Inc., is called *Elementary Mathematics Classroom Learning System*. This program provides practice and good feedback on math skills from single digit addition to complex division and fractions. Its record keeping and individualization features are primitive when compared to the math curriculums available for larger computers, although it does offer some degree of individualized practice and feedback. Like many of the newer programs available with micros, the graphics that are used to maintain interest are much better than those available with the older math software.

Probably the most elaborate use of the graphics capabilities of the new micro-systems appears in a series of math drill and practice programs called *Arcademic Skill Builders* that are offered by Developmental Learning Materials (DLM). These programs provide practice in basic computational skills in an arcade game format designed to hold children's interest in much the same way that video games do. In a recent pilot study (Weinstock, Torgesen, Jones, & Rashotte, 1983), we compared the effectiveness of DLM's program for addition skills with that of a standard drill program that did not employ elaborate graphics. Over a three week period in which learning disabled children practiced with either program for ten minutes a day, the programs were equally effective in increasing the number of problems children could complete successfully within a given period of time. Although the children enjoyed the DLM program more than the standard drill and practice format, they become bored with both programs after about two weeks.

Again, although the DLM programs employ state-of-the-art graphics and animation features, they do not have the kind of record keeping features that allow truly individualized practice, and they require the teacher to coordinate distribution of practice among different skills. Thus, even though we are much closer to having good software available in basic skills than even a year ago, and each of the programs discussed here has many features to recommend its use, we are still some distance away from having both hardware and software systems than can provide maximum advantages of CAI for mildly handicapped children. This is not to suggest that current systems cannot be used effectively, but simply to point out that systems now in use do not provide a good indication of what CAI with mildly handicapped children can become over the next several years.

NEEDS FOR THE PRESENT AND FUTURE

The ultimate effectiveness of CAI in helping to remediate the academic problems of mildly handicapped children will, of course, depend upon much more than improvements in computer technology. There are at least three kinds of factors that will influence developments in this area. These factors include: (1) training and adjustment of teachers to computers; (2) availability and service delivery systems; and (3) developments in instructional software and hardware. I will briefly indicate some general requirements in each of these areas.

First, teachers must be trained so that they understand both the capabilities and limitations of computer technology. Until now, the emphasis has been on tailoring software to teacher needs, but it also appears likely that teachers will need to alter some of the ways they teach in order to take more complete advantage of the computer's supplementary role. Teachers do not need to be computer programmers, but they must develop confidence in operating computers and an understanding of their capabilities so that they can think of CAI as an integral part of their overall instructional program rather than as simply a "fun" activity or enrichment device.

Just as there is a smaller student-teacher ratio for mildly handicapped children than normal children, there may also need to be a smaller student-computer ratio in resource rooms than regular classrooms. This is particularly true if we focus on computers as an aid in acquisition of basic tool skills in academic subjects. Children who learn normally do not need extensive computer time to practice basic skills in the same manner as mildly handicapped children. We have recently completed a one and a half year project to develop use of computers in a resource room serving learning disabled and mildly mentally retarded children (Young, Torgesen, Rashotte, & Jones, 1983). It is our estimate that these children need a minimum of one half hour a day on the computer to broadly affect their academic skills. If the average resource room serves 30 children a day, that means that approximately three computers are required for each resource room. Although schools have been purchasing computers in record numbers, we are a long way from having the service delivery capacity that will allow computers to be used as an integral part of instruction for mildly handicapped children.

Finally, we must await the development of better software, and perhaps more capable hardware, to provide fully adequate CAI in resource rooms. While there are many elements involved in the production of effective software, at least two stand out as of primary importance. First, software that is designed to enhance functioning in basic academic skills should require mastery of component skills based on both speed and accuracy criteria. The measure of speed of responding is crucial in the area of component skills because these skills must be executed with relative ease if they are to be integrated smoothly in more complex activities. Second, a computer curriculum must be designed so that it can be integrated easily with teacher directed activities. A number of the larger software developers are now making efforts to integrate their computer offerings with their traditional curriculum materials, but this needs to be done more effectively.

Over the next several years, the expanding memory and processing speed of microcomputers should be able to support software that can sensitively adapt itself to the instructional needs of each child. At that time, we may begin to realize the oft-stated but infrequently realized goal of individualized instruction for all children with learning handicaps.

REFERENCES

Berliner, D. C., & Rosenshine, B. (1977). The acquisition of knowledge in the classroom. In R. C. Anderson, R. J. Spiro, & W. E. Montague (Eds.), *Schooling and the acquisition of knowledge.* Hillsdale, New Jersey: Lawrence Erlbaum Associates.

Campione, J. C., & Brown, A. L. (1978). Toward a theory of intelligence: Contributions from research with retarded children. *Intelligence, 2,* 279-304.

Dence, M. (1980). Toward defining the role of CAI: A review. *Educational Technology,* 50-54.

Deshler, D. D., Schumaker, J. B., & Lenz, B. K. (in press). Academic and cognitive interventions for LD adolescents: Part I. *Journal of Learning Disabilities.*

Deshler, D. D., Schumaker, J. B., Lenz, B. K., & Ellis, E. (in press). Academic and cognitive interventions for LD adolescents: Part II. *Journal of Learning Disabilities.*

Edwards, G., Norton, S., Taylor, S., Weiss, M., & Van Dusseldorf, R. (1975). How effective is CAI? A review of the research. *Education Leadership, 33*(2), 147-153.

Fletcher, J. D. (1979). Computer-assisted instruction in beginning reading: The Stanford Projects. In L. Resnick & P. Weaver (Eds.), *Theory and practice of early reading.* Hillsdale, New Jersey: Lawrence Erlbaum Associates.

Fletcher, J. D., & Atkinson, R. C. (1972). Evaluation of the Stanford CAI Program in initial reading. *Journal of Educational Psychology, 63*(6), 597-602.

Fletcher, J. D. & Suppes, P. (1972). Computer assisted instruction in reading: Grades 4-6. *Educational Technology,* 45-49.

Foster, K., & Torgesen, J. K. (1983). *The influence of computer-assisted instruction and workbook practice on the learning of multiplication facts by learning disabled children.* Unpublished manuscript, Florida State University.

Hallahan, D. P., & Kauffman, J. M. (1976). *Introduction to learning disabilities: A psychobehavioral approach.* Englewood Cliffs, New Jersey: Prentice-Hall.

Hallworth, H. J., & Brebner, A. (1980, April). *CAI for the developmentally handicapped: Nine years of progress.* Paper presented at the Association for the Development of the Computer-Based Instructional Systems, Washington, D. C. (ERIC Document Reproduction Service No. 198-792).

Hammill, E., & Bartel, N. R. (1975). *Teaching children with learning and behavior problems.* Boston: Allyn & Bacon.

Holland, P. W. (1980, April). *Computer-assisted instruction: A longitudinal study.* Panel presentation at the AERA Annual Conference.

Jamison, D., Fletcher, J. D., Suppes, P., & Atkinson, R. C. (1975). Cost and performance of computer assisted instruction for compensatory education. In R. Radner & J. Froomkim (Eds.), *Education as an industry.* New York: Columbia University Press.

Jamison, D. P., Suppes, P., & Wells, S. (1974). The effectiveness of alternate instructional media: A survey. *Review of Educational Research, 44,* 1-67.

Lepper, M. R. (1982, August). *Microcomputers in education: Motivational and social issues.* Paper presented at the annual meeting of the American Psychological Association, Washington, D. C.

Lesgold, A. M. (1983). A rationale for computer-based reading instruction. In A. C. Wilkenson (Ed.), *Classroom computers and cognitive science.* New York: Academic Press.

Lesgold, A. M., & Resnick, L. B. (1982). How reading difficulties develop: Perspectives from a longitudinal study. In J. P. Das, R. F. Mulcahy, & A. E. Wall (Eds.), *Theory and research in learning disabilities.* New York: Plenum Press.

Maxwell, M. (1980). *Improving student learning skills.* San Francisco: Jossey-Bass Publishers.

Resnick, L. B. (1981). The psychology of drill and practice. In L. B. Resnick & W. W. Ford (Eds.), *The psychology of mathematics for instruction.* Hillsdale, New Jersey: Lawrence Erlbaum Associates.

Roblyer, M. D., & King, F. J. (1983, January). *Reasonable expectations for computer-based instruction in basic reading skills.* Paper presented at the meetings of the Association for Educational Communication and Technology.

Schiffman, G., Tobin, D., & Buchanan, B. (1982). Microcomputer instruction for the learning disabled. *Journal of Learning Disabilities, 15,* 557-559.

Stanovich, K. E. (1982b). Individual differences in the cognitive processes of reading II: Text-level processes. *Journal of Learning Disabilities, 15,* 549-554.

Suppes, P., Jerman, M. & Brian, D. (1968). *Computer-assisted instruction: Stanford's 1965-1966 arithmetic program.* New York, London: Academic Press.

Suppes, P., & Morningstar, M. (1969). Computer-assisted instruction. *Science, 166,* 343-350.

Tait, K., Hartley, J., & Anderson, R. C. (1974). Feedback procedures in computer-assisted arithmetic instruction. *British Journal of Educational Psychology, 43*(2), 161-171.

Torgesen, J. K., & Licht, B. (1983). The learning disabled child as an inactive learner: Retrospect and prospects. In J. D. McKinney & L. Feagons (Eds.), *Topics in learning disabilities, Vol. 1.* Rockville, Maryland: Aspen Press.

Torgesen, J. K., & Young, K. (1983). Priorities for the use of microcomputers with learning disabled children. *Journal of Learning Disabilities.*

Weinstock, S., Torgesen, J. K., Jones, K. M., & Rashotte, C. A. (1983). A comparison between two drill programs on addition facts with learning disabled children. Unpublished manuscript, Florida State University.

Wilkenson, A. C. (1983). Learning to read in real time. In A. C. Wilkenson (Ed.), *Classroom computers and cognitive science.* New York: Academic Press.

Young, K., Torgesen, J. K., Rashotte, C. A., & Jones, K. M. (1983). *Microcomputers in the resource room: A handbook for teachers.* Leon County Public Schools, Tallahassee, Florida.

Microcomputer Technology and Related Services

Roland K. Yoshida

ABSTRACT. Innovations in microcomputer technology in the area of related services (e.g., communication therapy, counseling, occupational and physical therapy) are appearing in ever-increasing numbers. This paper describes several of these innovations and attempts to analyze their potential contribution in helping the handicapped to function more independently. The innovations are discussed according to a cost/benefit approach. Costs associated with these innovations include those for conducting studies to determine the efficacy of the innovation; purchasing new or modified hardware (microprocessors, peripheral devices) and software; training personnel to modify software for unique needs and to instruct potential clients on the uses of the innovations; and devoting storage space for hardware and software as well as providing for their maintenance. Potential benefits include the number of handicapped individuals to be served; number of functions and tasks to be performed and the efficiency in performing them; and the perceived degree of independence to be achieved by students and clients.

Regardless of the newspaper, popular magazine or professional journal, articles describing microcomputers make these new machines seem indispensable for daily living. Microcomputers are said to help adults increase their work productivity through the use of easy-to-learn programs. One of the most frequently advertised applications is word processing. Time consuming manuscript corrections are eliminated because editorial changes can be made by using the unique commands of a particular word processing program

---

Requests for reprints should be sent to: Roland K. Yoshida, Department of Special Education, Graduate School of Education, Fordham University at Lincoln Center, 113 W. 60th Street, New York, NY 10023.

© 1984 by The Haworth Press, Inc. All rights reserved.

with the desired text. Programs are also available to teach languages, mathematics, social sciences, and business at levels appropriate for children and adults. There are even programs for the hobbyist, such as stamp collecting, keeping track of football statistics, and of course, the ever-popular computer games. Although these programs show the versatility of microcomputers, they have a single theme in common: tremendous potential to enhance people's level of independence in employment and in their personal lives.

Increasing the level of independent living is also the primary goal of any educational or rehabilitation program for the handicapped. Consequently, this goal is directing the efforts of researchers interested in improving the quality of related services provided to the handicapped. This paper will focus on technology related to communication and to physical and occupational therapies which help the handicapped child or adult participate in learning situations or in daily living activities. For example, non-vocal, physically involved individuals may not be able to utter sounds or write a message to express themselves. McFarland (1981) designed a system which uses a Radio Shack microcomputer and voice synthesizer. Users develop a dictionary of common phrases and sentences which are coded according to a standard numeric computer code termed ASCII. When the user wants to communicate a desired message, the user presses buttons that translate the ASCII characters to phonemes which are converted to spoken language by the voice synthesizer. Users who are so motorically involved that they cannot use the keyboard can activate the voice synthesizer using a biofeedback device that is linked to the computer. This device can be used to select phrases on the TV monitor by moving a forearm or other muscle to signal that that phrase should be spoken. Such devices can enable those who cannot speak to carry on a relatively normal telephone conversation (McFarland, 1981).

This is but one example of the numerous innovations being reported in the popular and professional literature. Like the microcomputer field in general, new ideas are rapidly being developed. The challenge to related service providers is selecting those innovations which are the most appropriate and cost-effective. In order to help potential users of these technological advances, this paper will (a) describe and categorize these innovations, and (b) propose some factors to consider when deciding whether an innovation is potentially cost-effective.

DESCRIPTION OF MICROCOMPUTER ADAPTATIONS

One conventional way of thinking about microcomputers is based upon systems analysis. Users *input* or enter information which microcomputers receive, and process. In turn, microcomputers *output* or give a response to users. For most people, microcomputers purchased off-the-shelf do not need modifications. With commercially available software, microcomputers can perform most desired operations such as word processing. Keyboards provided with the machines enable users to enter information and instructions into the computer's memory. Output is presented on the TV monitor or usually printed on widely available dot-matrix or letter-quality printers.

However, what happens when users either cannot easily strike keyboards or read information from monitors or printers? These are the questions posed to inventors; their solutions are described below. The next two sections primarily describe hardware or equipment used in conjunction with microcomputers; in computer jargon these are called peripheral devices. The reader should keep in mind that computers must also be programmed to interpret information received from and sent to these peripheral devices. Thus, for most of these peripheral devices, "translator" software packages must be developed and purchased.

Input Innovations

For the deaf and hard-of-hearing, computer technology is increasing the capabilities of teletype (TTY) systems. TTYs have been used in communicating with and among the deaf for many years. In order to use TTYs, all parties in a conversation must own a TTY and a modem, which translates information from the electronic impulses used by the computer to sound that can be sent across telephone lines. This situation greatly limits the group of people with whom those dependent on TTYs can communicate. Several innovations are being developed which (a) enable TTY and microcomputer owners to communicate with hearing persons who do not own or have access to such equipment (Glaser, 1981; Johnson & Hagstad, 1981), (b) allow different communication systems such as the TTY and the microcomputer to be compatible with one another (Bozzuto, 1981), and (c) make TTYs more portable by reducing them to the form of pocket computers (Levitt, 1981). For example, Glaser

(1981) invented what he terms a message converter (a metal box containing electronic components such as a microprocessor and the necessary software) which allows TTY operators to converse with persons who own only a telephone. A touch tone telephone is preferred because telephone signals are more easily sent in this manner, but tone encoders are commercially available to supplement those who own rotary dial equipment. Communication is accomplished by the user dialing the appropriate numbers which correspond to a predetermined code. The message converter translates these codes into the alphabet or number system and displays the message on a remote TTY or on a remote computer monitor. A deaf person at the remote TTY or computer can then respond orally, or through pre-recorded messages. Although TTY owners must buy some hardware and software, and non-TTY owners must learn a new coding system, this innovation clearly extends the capability of the deaf to communicate with those who do not own, or probably will not buy, TTYs or microcomputers in the near future.

Rather than being dependent on cumbersome machines such as TTYs or desk-top microcomputers, Levitt (1981) suggested using an easily transportable communication system at comparable or less cost than a TTY. The basic components of this system include Radio Shack's TRS-80 pocket computer and an inexpensive modem; peripheral devices such as a miniature line printer and cassette tape recorder for data storage can augment this system. The basic system can be used like a conventional TTY in which typed messages can be sent and received. A template fits over the pocket computer's keyboard in order to help the user press TTY compatible keys. In addition, because the heart of the system is a computer, it can perform like an intelligent terminal in which frequently used messages can be transmitted by pressing a single button.

Another major information inputting challenge is helping motorically involved persons who experience difficulty with speaking, holding objects, or striking the standard keyboard. Depending upon the nature and degree of involvement, motorically involved persons can send commands to the computer by (a) using templates that fit over a standard keyboard and eliminate the need to operate two keys simultaneously (Prentke Romich Inc., no date); (b) increasing the space between keys to 2 inches (EKEG Electronics Co., no date-a); (c) using the "joy sticks" employed in computer games (Schwejda & McDonald, 1981); (d) repositioning their eyes (Friedman, Kiliany, Dzmura, & Anderson, 1981), body (Goldenberg, 1981) or head

(Jaffe, 1981); (e) speaking into microphones which translate voice commands into electronic impulses (Henle, 1981); Launey, 1981; Scott Instruments, no date; Springer, 1981); (f) using an optical bar code reader to identify grocery products and prices (Hardin, 1981; Probst, 1981); and (g) using push-button, breath, foot-pedal, remote-control, muscle-flex, jaw-breaker, knee, or photoelectric switches (Cannon, 1981; EKEG Electronics Co., no date-b; Fisher, 1981; Gale, no date; Gaylord, Smith & Beak, 1981; Rowell & Dalrymple, 1981; Schwejda, no date; TASH, no date). All of the above innovations generally use commercially available hardware.

The final example in this section concerns the Kurzweil (1981) Reading Machine (KRM). The KRM is custom designed as a self-contained unit that electronically scans printed and typewritten material of any size. The KRM transmits this information to a microprocessor which computes the pronunciation of the text, and reproduces the text auditorially. The listener can control the reading rate, adjust the tonality of the voice (which speaks at 1 1/2 times normal speech rates), repeat selected lines or words, among other functions. With this machine, blind persons do not have to depend upon readers or limit themselves to tape recorded materials or those reproduced in braille.

Output Innovations

Several innovators have used commercially available voice synthesizers made by VOTRAX (Blazie, 1981; Hallenbeck, 1981), and Radio Shack (McFarland, 1981) to adapt the microcomputer's output to the sensory capabilities of the handicapped user. Rather than using a scanning glass plate as with the KRM, Blazie's (1981) system named Total Talk (Maryland Computer Services, no date), uses a keyboard for inputting data into a microcomputer. The microprocessor is programmed to convert information into digital codes corresponding to 64 different phonemes which employ English speaking rules. Any input can be converted to speech; thus, the system is not restricted by a particular set of words or phrases. Complementing voice synthesizers are large-print monitors which are used as part of a computer system for partially sighted individuals (National Institute for Rehabilitation Engineering, no date). In short, voice synthesizers and large print monitors expand the visually handicapped person's access to printed materials and commercially available software.

Examples of Innovative Software

Besides developing software programs to help operate peripheral devices, innovators have been concerned with writing software to increase the capability of microcomputers to serve particular groups of handicapped people. For example, word processing is one of the most used programs for microcomputers. For the visually handicapped, Holladay (1981) and Stepp (1981) reported on similar braille word processing systems which are designed to eliminate the costly process of rebrailling a page when an error is found. Both systems have the capability of using an Apple microcomputer's keyboard for entering text which is then translated into the appropriate braille code. Small sections of the text can be displayed on a TV monitor for proofreading and editing before being typed out in braille. These advances free the braillist from working with a system which includes a brailler. Both Holladay (1981) and Stepp (1981) suggest that, if braillists could have access to microcomputers, they could type at home and their work could be sent on diskette to a central location for brailling. With some modifications to this software, it is conceivable that diskettes could be sent directly to handicapped users who own microcomputers and voice synthesizers for immediate use.

We have already discussed how innovators have modified or bypassed keyboards for inputting information. For non-verbal, physically involved persons, however, the use of modified input systems of the type discussed in this paper remains time consuming and tiring because users still must enter each letter and word in a sentence. Hillinger, Fox, and Wilson (1981) and Till and Maier (1981) have developed software programs to make communication more efficient for these persons. In particular, Hillinger et al. (1981) have developed a software program based upon generative grammar principles which expands telegraphic sentences into grammatically acceptable sentences. Users scan the TV monitor and choose sentences by pressing a button for the desired sentence subjects. The procedure is repeated for predicates, modifiers, and objects. The program prompts users to select whether sentences will be simple or complex, interrogative, negative, emphatic, or in the past tense. With this information, the program generates grammatically appropriate sentences which can be displayed on TV monitors, or spoken if voice synthesizers are attached to the microcomputer.

COST/BENEFIT ANALYSIS AND MICROCOMPUTER INNOVATIONS

The preceding discussion shows the considerable strides made to improve the handicapped person's capability for independent living. However, potential users with limited resources must choose the most appropriate microcomputer, peripheral device, and associated software from among many attractive alternatives. Although there is no singularly right way to evaluate these alternatives, a cost/benefit approach may prove helpful.

Several assumptions are incorporated into the approach. First, the approach assumes that potential users do not desire a precise dollar statement of cost/benefit. Rather, this model attempts to alert users to important issues which should be considered in purchase decisions. For example, how much time (and therefore cost) will it take to train staff in the use of the particular innovation? Second, in order to use the model properly, all desired information must be available. However, formal evaluations of the efficacy of the peripheral devices or software were rarely presented in the reports of innovations discussed in this paper. Such omissions are problematic when evaluating hardware and software products. In the absence of this information, users will have to conduct their own preliminary evaluation of an innovation. Finally, no variable weighs as heavily as the needs of users. Nevertheless, the model will help guide the selection of an innovation as well as help plan for its most effective use.

Cost Variables

Evaluation of Innovations. A popular belief is that evaluations should be done *after* users have purchased equipment or software and have used it for a period of time. However, holding to this belief will lead to some costly mistakes. To prevent such mistakes, thorough investigations of various innovations are needed by the handicapped user *before* a purchase is made. For the innovations reviewed in this paper, little independent research about the efficacy of the innovations was available. Perhaps purchasers can begin insisting that independent evaluations be conducted and results reported. This suggestion is a costly one for inventors; therefore, compliance with such a request may be minimal. An alternative approach would be to devote space in professional journals for reviews of various innovations. However, many innovations will go unreported and those that are given journal space will appear with the usual publication delay. Given these conditions, purchasers not only must read about innovations but also must insist that inventors allow them to pilot test particular innovations with the intended client population. Although purchasers must ultimately bear the costs of such evaluations, these costs are insignificant if they avoid errors and result in buying the right equipment or computer programs.

Purchase of Hardware and Software. This is the dollar price for obtaining hardware and software. In making comparative judgments about systems, two considerations should be kept in mind. The microcomputer market is clearly undergoing a dialectical process of growth which complicates product selection. New manufacturers and programming companies appear with such frequency that their names are rarely recognized. While this is evidence for optimism about the future of microcomputers, a complementary force exists which is standardizing the industry and reducing the number of companies. A classic example is the rapid acceptance of the IBM Personal Computer which pressured many companies into manufacturing compatible hardware and software. What will happen to companies who do not conform to IBM standards?

A complementary example concerns Osborne, the pioneer in developing portable computers that is now bankrupt. Where will users find new programs compatible with this system; where can they purchase replacement parts and secure maintenance services on these machines? This discussion does not imply that new and experimental systems should not be bought; they may be exactly what the service provider or handicapped user needs. However, buyers should be aware that unless they assess whether a manufacturer will remain in the industry mainstream, they may not be able to maintain their equipment and will more than likely lose flexibility in upgrading or adapting their systems to future development.

Another consideration concerns the extent to which an innovation maximizes the use of previously purchased equipment. For example, in the section on input innovations, several relatively simple devices which capitalized upon TTYs were described. With Glaser's (1981) message converter, a person owning only a telephone could communicate with a deaf TTY operator. Bozzuto (1981) developed a modem so that users owning equipment that transmitted data at different speeds, such as TTYs and microcomputers, could communicate with one another. For some users, buying the most technologically advanced system is a goal in itself; however, many users are unable to purchase state-of-the-art equipment. For these users, searching for innovations that make use of already-available equipment is an important consideration.

Training of Personnel. An often overlooked item is the amount of time needed to train personnel in the use of a particular innovation. Regardless of how simple and familiar microcomputer technology may appear to some, learning about its capabilities is analogous to learning a new language. I have found that the frequent users of microcomputers are those teachers who had previously been exposed to computers (a) as part of their undergraduate or graduate training, (b) through employment experiences, or (c) for personal interest, either as an outside leisure activity or for managing home financial and bookkeeping tasks. In most cases, these teachers had taken some formal training in the computer's use. I have also observed situations in which microcomputers merely occupied space or were ineffectively used; in these cases, staff had very little systematic exposure to microcomputers. In short, staff must be trained if microcomputers are to be used effectively. Training adds to the cost of any innovation.

Storage and Maintenance. The cost of keeping microcomputers and various peripheral devices in proper working order is an item that should not be overlooked. A microcomputer with a disk drive and printer occupies at least one fullsize office desk. With additional peripheral devices such as telephone modems (Buzzuto, 1981), message converters (Glaser, 1981), and braille printers (Holladay, 1981), additional space has to be assigned. If several microcomputers are located in a single room, electrical re-wiring of the room may be necessary to provide enough outlets to power the machines and to reduce circuit overload. Finally, regardless of the quality and reputation of a particular microcomputer system, users will have to anticipate spending money to repair or replace equipment, as well as losing valuable time in meeting program or personal goals due to equipment malfunction.

Benefit Variables

Estimated Number of Users to Be Served and Frequency of Use. In making decisions about a particular innovation, cost factors have to be weighed against benefit variables. The most obvious benefit variable is the number of potential users for an innovation. For example, Kurzweil (1982) estimates that 3,000 persons use the 300 Kurzweil Reading Machines (KRM) in the field. Because the price of a KRM ranges from $22,000 to $29,000, the price per user is about $2,000 to $3,000. However, users are not typically evenly distributed in geographical areas. In some cases, there may be only one potential user for a machine, thus increasing the cost/benefit figure dramatically.

Identifying potential users produces only a partial picture of benefit. We usually presume that all potential users will take full advantage of the innovation. However, some users may find that an innovation does not quite meet their needs or that it is inconvenient to use. In such cases, expressing cost-effectiveness in terms of the number of potential users may be misleading. In short, the decision-maker must account for frequency of use in assessing the benefits of an innovation.

Number of Functions and Tasks. Although an innovation is developed for a specific purpose, some innovations are more versatile than others. For example, some input systems for motorically involved persons are limited to just one mode such as the "joy stick," while others were designed with the accompanying software to handle various options. Given the particular client population, having a range of options greatly increases the probability that the system will attract a wider audience. Again, this is but one variable to consider; gaining this flexibility may also be prohibitively expensive.

Perceived Degree of Independence. This factor can be analyzed in two ways. First, the overriding consideration in purchasing hardware and software is curricula; microcomputer technology is only a vehicle, albeit a powerful one, for helping handicapped persons achieve independent living. On the basis of curricular fit, decision-makers can prioritize and justify their product selections. For visually handicapped persons, is it more important to buy voice synthesizing systems to help in reading text (Blazie, 1981; Maryland Computer Services, no date) or light sensitive bar code readers to identify grocery products and their prices (Hardin, 1981; Probst, 1981)? Given limited dollars, comparative judgments may have to be made. Decision-makers must review curricula to help them determine which innovation better fits the needs of the target group.

Another analysis of perceived independence is the extent to which innovations reduce the dependence of handicapped persons on the school and agency personnel. For example, visually handicapped persons can use the Kurzweil Reading Machine rather than a reader.

Voice synthesizers can help motorically involved persons communicate more quickly and more precisely with others. Complementing the decrease in clients' dependence is the increase in efficient staff use. Instruction and rehabilitation are labor intensive activities. Several of the innovations mentioned in this paper free staff so that they can either assist more clients or perform other important activities such as program planning.

CONCLUSION

We are witnessing the rapid adaptation of the microcomputer to the related service needs of handicapped persons. The innovations discussed in this paper are probably no longer the state of the art; they may have already given way to new approaches and concepts. As these and other innovations gain wider publicity and popular acclaim (as witnessed in recent articles appearing in the *New York Times Sunday Magazine* [Cherry & Cherry, 1984] and *Smithsonian* [Trachtman, 1984]), potential users are cautioned to be deliberate in making purchase decisions. It is not technology per se that is important. The primary question is whether, within cost/benefit limits, technology helps handicapped individuals achieve important educational or rehabilitation goals; that is, improves their attainment of independent living.

REFERENCES

Blazie, D. B. (1981). TOTAL TALK—A computer terminal for the blind. *Proceedings of the Johns Hopkins first national search for applications of personal computing to aid the handicapped* (pp. 251-254). New York: Institute of Electrical and Electronics Engineers (IEEE).

Bozzuto, R. C. (1981). The universal translating modem: An advanced telecommunication device for the deaf. *Proceedings of the Johns Hopkins first national search for applications of personal computing to aid the handicapped* (pp. 62-64). New York: IEEE.

Cannon, T. W. (1981). An optically actuated keyboard system. *Proceedings of the Johns Hopkins first national search for applications of personal computing to aid the handicapped* (pp. 186-189). New York: IEEE.

Cherry, L., & Cherry, R. (1984). New hope for the disabled. *New York Times Sunday Magazine,* February 5, 52-60.

EKEG Electronics Co. Ltd. (no date). Expanded keyboard for Apple. In G. C. Vanderheiden and L. M. Walstead (Eds.), *International Software-Hardware Registry.* Madison, WI: Trace Research and Development Center. (a)

EKEG Electronics Co. Ltd. (no date). Remote keyboard for Apple. In G. C. Vanderheiden and L. M. Walstead (Eds.), *International Software-Hardware Registry.* Madison, WI: Trace Research and Development Center. (b)

Fisher, J. S. (1981). Menu assisted data entry system: Keyboardless interaction with the personal computer. *Proceedings of the Johns Hopkins first national search for applications of personal computing to aid the handicapped* (pp. 169-174). New York: IEEE.

Friedman, M. B., Kiliany, G., Dzmura, M., & Anderson, D. (1981). The eyetracker communication system. *Proceedings of the Johns Hopkins first national search for applications of personal computing to aid the handicapped* (pp. 183-185). New York: IEEE.

Gale, M. (no date). Compudapter. In G. C. Vanderheiden, and L. M. Walstead. *International software-hardware registry*. Madison, WI: Trace Research and Develoment Center.

Gaylord, A. S., Smith, S., & Beak, P. (1981). Text writing, speaking, and appliance control for the severely physically handicapped. *Proceedings of the Johns Hopkins first national search for applications of personal computing to aid the handicapped* (pp. 178-180). New York: IEEE.

Glaser, R. E. (1981). A telephone communication aid for the deaf. *Proceedings of the Johns Hopkins first national search for applications of personal computing to aid the handicapped* (pp. 11-15). New York: IEEE.

Goldenberg, E. P. (1981). Flexible band width communication for motorically impaired persons. *Proceedings of the Johns Hopkins first national search for applications of personal computing to aid the handicapped* (pp. 190-192). New York: IEEE.

Hallenbeck, C. E. (1981). KANSYS, the Kansas system: Full speech operating system for blind computer users. *Proceedings of the Johns Hopkins first national search for applications of personal computing to aid the handicapped* (pp. 220-223). New York: IEEE.

Hardin, J. C. (1981). Content identification for the blind. *Proceedings of the Johns Hopkins first national search for applications of personal computers to aid the handicapped* (p. 226). New York. IEEE.

Henle, R. A. (1981). Electronic keyboard. *Proceedings of the Johns Hopkins first national search for applications of personal computing to aid the handicapped* (pp. 146-150). New York: IEEE.

Hillinger, M., Fox, B., & Wilson, M. (1981). Computer-enhanced communication systems for the Apple II. *Proceedings of the Johns Hopkins first national search for applications of personal computing to aid the handicapped* (pp. 16-18). New York: IEEE.

Holladay, D. (1981). BRAILLE-EDIT program connecting an Apple II computer with a VersaBraille paperless brailler. *Proceedings of the Johns Hopkins first national search for applications of personal computing to aid the handicapped* (pp. 231-233). New York: IEEE.

Jaffe, D. L. (1981). An ultrasonic head position interface for wheelchair control. *Proceedings of the Johns Hopkins first national search for applications of personal computing to aid the handicapped* (pp. 142-145). New York: IEEE.

Johnson, A. B., & Hagstad, R. F. (1981). DTMF telecommunications for the deaf and speech-impaired. *Proceedings of the Johns Hopkins first national search for applications of personal computing to aid the handicapped* (pp. 29-32). New York: IEEE.

Johnston, D. K. (1981). DEAFSIGN: A series of computerized instructional programs for the teaching of sign language. *Proceedings of the Johns Hopkins first national search for applications of personal computing to aid the handicapped* (pp. 65-66). New York: IEEE.

Kurzweil, R. C. (1982). Kurzweil reading machine for the blind. *Proceedings of the Johns Hopkins first national search for applications of personal computing to aid the handicapped* (pp. 236-241). New York: IEEE.

Launey, R. O. (1981). The motor-handicapped support system. *Proceedings of the Johns Hopkins first national search for applications of personal computing to aid the handicapped* (pp. 104-109). New York: IEEE.

Levitt, H. (1981). A pocket telecommunicator for the deaf. *Proceedings of the Johns Hopkins first national search for applications of personal computing to aid the handicapped* (pp. 39-42). New York: IEEE.

Macurik, K. (1981). A vocalization trainer for the hearing impaired. *Proceedings of the Johns Hopkins first national search for applications of personal computing to aid the handicapped.* (pp. 2-3). New York: IEEE.

Maryland Computer Services. (no date). Total Talk. In G. C. Vanderheiden and L. M. Walstead (Eds.), *International software-hardware registry*. Madison, WI: Trace Research and Development Center.

McFarland, W. D. (1981). A communications aid for the non-oral severely disabled. *Proceedings of the John Hopkins first national search for applications of personal computing to aid the handicapped* (pp. 19-20). New York: IEEE.

National Institute for Rehabilitation Engineering. (no date). Large type. In G. C. Vanderheiden and L. M. Walstead (Eds.), *International software-hardware registry*. Madison, WI: Trace Research and Development Center.

Prentke Romich Company. (no date). Apple keyboard interface (AKI-1). In G. C. Vanderheiden and L. M. Walstead (Eds.), *International software-hardware registry*. Madison, WI: Trace Research and Development Center.

Probst, R. J. (1981). The B-A-R, A device designed to aid the visually handicapped. *Proceedings of the Johns Hopkins first national search for applications of personal computing to aid the handicapped* (pp. 234-235). New York: IEEE.

Rowell, D., & Dalrymple, G. F. (1981). The UNICOM: A microprocessor based communicator for the non-vocal severely motor impaired. *Proceedings of the Johns Hopkins first national search for applications of personal computing to aid the handicapped* (pp. 152-156). New York: IEEE.

Schwejda, P. (no date). Adaptive firmware card. In G. C. Vanderheiden and L. M. Walstead (Eds.), *International hardware-software registry*. Madison, WI: Trace Research and Development Center.

Schwejda, P., & McDonald, J. (1981). Adapting the Apple for physically handicapped users: Two different solutions. *Proceedings of the Johns Hopkins first national search for applications of personal computing to aid the handicapped* (pp. 52-55). New York: IEEE.

Scott Instruments. (no date). Shadow/Vet. In G. C. Vanderheiden and L. M. Walstead (Eds.), *International hardware-software registry*. Madison, WI: Trace Research and Development Center.

Springer, A. E. (1981). Microcomputer based verbal exchange for the handicapped. *Proceedings of the Johns Hopkins first national search for applications of personal computing to aid the handicapped* (pp. 93-95). New York: IEEE.

Stepp, R. (1981). A Braille word processing system. *Proceedings of the Johns Hopkins first national search for applications of personal computing to aid the handicapped* (pp. 202-204). New York: IEEE.

TASH. Target (No. 2410). In G. C. Vanderheiden and L. M. Walstead (Eds.), *International hardware-software registry*. Madison, WI: Trace Research and Development Center.

Till, J.A., & Maier, M. F. (1981). Numbered-accessed expressive language program. *Proceedings of the Johns Hopkins first national search for applications of personal computing to aid the handicapped* (pp. 27-28). New York: IEEE.

Trachtman, P. (1984). Putting computers into the hands of children without language. *Smithsonian, 14*(11), 42-51.

Welsh, A. J., Mancuso, T. G., & Licata, S. P. (1981). Computer assisted instruction in expressive and receptive fingerspelling. *Proceedings of Johns Hopkins first national search for applications of personal computing to aid the handicapped* (pp. 56-58). New York: IEEE.

Training Special Education Personnel for Effective Use of Microcomputer Technology: Critical Needs and Directions

Melvyn I. Semmel
Merith A. Cosden
Dorothy S. Semmel
Eve Kelemen

ABSTRACT. Special educators have been quick to embrace microcomputer instruction; both special education and microcomputer instruction share the promise of developing individualized instructional programs matched to student needs. From this viewpoint, microcomputers have the potential for operationally defining what is "special" about special education. Despite this promise, however, there is a limited data base from which to make empirical decisions on effective microcomputer use in the classroom and on teacher training needs. A model for assessing teacher training needs is discussed in which microcomputer skills are viewed within the context of other teacher-effectiveness variables. A two-tiered approach to teacher training in microcomputer instruction is developed, based on the promise of microcomputer instruction and upon pragmatic classroom considerations.

The diffusion of microcomputer technology in our nation's schools has been referred to as a revolutionary innovation with promise for permanently affecting the scope and nature of education for all children (Papert, 1980). The new technology is being promoted as a principal vehicle through which pupil variance in rate and level of

---

Requests for reprints should be sent to: Melvyn I. Semmel, Department of Special Education, University of California-Santa Barbara, Santa Barbara, California 93106.
This paper was supported in part by a grant from the U.S. Department of Education, Office of Special Education and Rehabilitation Services, G0083-02860, to Project TEECh, Technology Effectiveness with Exceptional Children.

© 1984 by The Haworth Press, Inc. All rights reserved.

learning will be markedly reduced. New machines and software are being advertised and marketed as the means for realizing the promises of a new era in education. Today, some decision makers stand on the sidelines, skeptical and cautious, remembering the "fads and fancies" of bygone years that reside unused in the cluttered corners of the schools. Others, heedless to caution and convinced of their purpose, are rushing headlong toward adoption of the new innovation. Many teachers, fueled by the powerful forces of the marketplace, frustrated by the critics of education, pressured by the need to be innovative, confused by the rhetoric of "hacker" colleagues and administrators, and threatened by their personal state of computer "illiteracy," may well feel like unwilling passengers on a juggernaut bound for an ill defined "promised land."

In the midst of this chaotic phase of the technology revolution in the schools, many special educators have aligned themselves with those proposing adoption of the new innovation. For the most part, they have embraced the principles propelling the new technological revolution in the schools with a decided optimism. Many of the promised effects of microcomputers are, after all, similar to those of special education. For years, the field has been hard pressed to operationally define that which is "special" about special education for mildly handicapped students. Generally, the field has been limited to demonstrable administrative arrangements (e.g., special classes, resource rooms) and a set of verbalized ideals in alluding to the salient defining features of the enterprise. Little wonder, then, that the prospect of the microcomputer applications to the education of handicapped children in the schools has stimulated so much interest among workers in the field. Our assessment of special education suggests that contemporary pronouncements of the inherent capabilities of microcomputers are virtually synonymous with many of the objectives which characterize the ideals of the field.

Special education and microcomputer applications share the common objective of catering to individual differences by providing effective and efficient instruction matched to the characteristics of learners. Both purport to provide carefully sequenced content, appropriate feedback, and consistent and accurate monitoring of pupil performance. They both seek to offer appropriate pacing of instruction, efficient, extrinsically motivating formats and to provide for data-based instructional decisions. Each is directed toward assuring unbiased, reliable, and valid evaluation of pupil progress, and providing individualized educational planning and instruction within the least restrictive, most normalized, educational environments. Hence, what is purported to be "special" about most special education programs may well be subsumed by the promised hardware and software capabilities of the new technology. Little wonder, then, that much of the literature on microcomputer applications in special education is highly optimistic.

Recently published reports offer substantial evidence that the schools are in fact rapidly acquiring microcomputers and are attempting to integrate them into varied instructional contexts. For example, the Johns Hopkins national survey (Becker, 1983) reported that a majority of the schools in the nation currently have at least one microcomputer. There was, however, relatively little evidence that microcomputers are being efficiently and effectively utilized by school personnel toward reaching educational objectives for mildly handicapped students. For example, the study found that older, brighter males tend to be designated as the primary users of microcomputers in classrooms (Becker, 1983). On the other hand, Sheingold, Kane, and Endereweit (1983) report that there is a tendency for teachers to allocate access to microcomputers to bright and to underachieving students—with the "average" student having relatively fewer opportunities to gain access to the technology. There is virtually no evidence on what handicapped pupils do with microcomputers once gaining access to them; nor is there a body of empirical findings on the educational effects of microcomputer use by mildly handicapped pupils in the schools (Semmel, Semmel, Cosden, Gerber, & Goldman, 1983). While the general professional literature is replete with testimonials lauding microcomputer applications in the schools, it appears reasonable at this time to conclude that the microcomputer revolution remains more a promise than a validated educational innovation. In this sense, the new technology shares a status somewhat similar to other contemporary special education practices (see Semmel, Gottlieb, & Robinson, 1979).

In our view, the ultimate success or demise of microcomputer applications is dependent upon the degree to which the technology is appropriately used by personnel most proximal to its intended applications. Hence, in special education contexts, we maintain that the effects of the technology on mildly handicapped students will be constrained by the extent to which teachers are computer literate and prepared to integrate the innovation into their ongoing educational programs. If microcomputer applications in special education are to approach their potential value, we must assess and integrate two factors: (1) the cognitive and personality attributes of the learner, and (2) the specific instructional characteristics of the instructional setting, which we have labelled the Micro/Educational Environment (MEE). As depicted in Figure 1, the MEE is defined by a number of contextual variables including the technological configuration of the microcomputers (e.g., types of hardware and its arrangement), the instructional content of the software and courseware, teacher effectiveness, the administrative arrangement (e.g., resource room, special day class), and the cognitive and personality characteristics of the target student and his or her peers. Definition and description of these environments enables one to specify the conditions under which particular microcomputer effects can be expected. This will also allow teachers to make an appropriate match between the cognitive and personality attributes of handicapped learners and the specific instructional characteristics of the student's MEE. Both variable clusters (student characteristics and MEE) must be conceptually and operationally integrated if the innovation is to endure as an important facet of what the field calls "special education." How this integration is realized is a central problem and challenge for personnel preparation in special education.

FACTORS INFLUENCING TEACHER UTILIZATION OF TECHNOLOGY

Our ultimate concern is to maximize the effects of technology applications in the education of mildly handicapped pupils. Specifically, we are interested in how the complex variables which intervene between the allocation of microcomputer resources to the schools and eventual educational effects on pupils are mediated by teacher related variables. Figure 1 presents a comprehensive causal path model developed to guide a recently funded research program designed to study the effects of microcomputer technology in special education contexts (Semmel et al., 1983). The path model displays the hypothesized distal and proximal causal chains involved in the allocation, delivery, and effects of technology on mildly handicapped pupils. For the purposes of the present discussion we focus attention on the variables associated with the teacher's effectiveness as a contributing factor in determining appropriate microeducational environments (MEEs) to which handicapped pupils gain access, use, and derive meaningful educational effects. Teacher effectiveness in influencing MEEs is viewed as being mediated through (a)

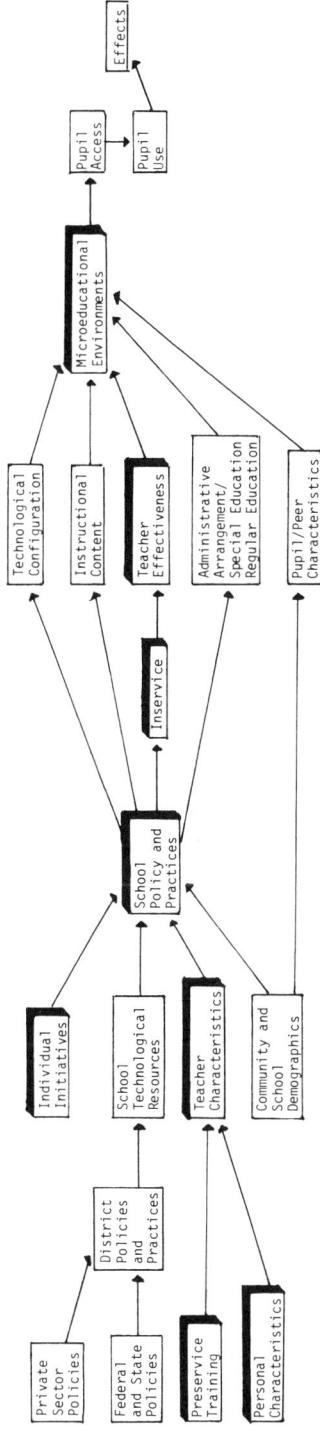

Figure 1. Path model of factors influencing teacher training, teacher effectiveness, and the microeducational environment in which mildly handicapped students receive their instruction.

the personal characteristics of teachers themselves, (b) school site formal and informal allocations of technical assistance or inservice training opportunities as determined by policy and other influences, (c) participation of teachers as members of formal and informal community-based microcomputer "User Groups," and (d) the history of teachers in preservice special education and computer literacy training programs as experienced in colleges and universities. By describing the factors that determine effective utilization of the new technology, areas of strength and weakness in personnel training can be empirically assessed. As described below, factors of concern include the selection criteria for teachers to receive training, administrative support and structure of inservice opportunities, local resources available to "user groups" and preservice teacher training opportunities.

Teacher Characteristics

The probability of adoption of microcomputer applications by teachers of handicapped children is, in part, a function of teacher intellectual curiosity, attitudes toward change, level of computer literacy, and other cognitive and personality variables. Individual differences among teachers with regard to these characteristics are attributable to innate factors, personal experiences, and the extent and nature of previous training. The readiness of teachers to adopt other innovations affecting educational practice are to a large extent dependent on similar variables. The acceptance of new technology is unique only to the extent that the implied personal commitments necessary for change are radically different from and demand greater relative response cost than other recent innovations in the schools.

Teachers with a history of aversion to machines, who tend to fear mathematics, who associate technology with anti-humanistic themes, who have a generally pessimistic view of their capabilities for learning completely new repertoires, who have limited confidence in handicapped children's abilities to learn, and who are committed to a particular instructional paradigm, can be expected to be the most resistant. Hence, important precursors to successful diffusion and adoption of microcomputer technology in special education are factors directly associated with teachers' personal/professional attitudes, perceptions of self and learners, cognitive characteristics, and personal experiences with technology.

The role of innate characteristics and formatively acquired personal attributes of teachers as predictors of the adoption of microcomputer technology is an issue of such magnitude as to fall beyond the scope of the present discussion. Suffice it to say that if teachers have had limited exposure to technology prior to entering the profession, then they will surely have less propensity to embrace the microcomputer revolution. If teachers enter special education programs with restrictive attitudes reflected in limited goals for handicapped children and rigidly adhere to their own preferred instructional paradigms, then they will surely limit the potential applications of microcomputer technology for their pupils.

It is obvious that teachers can be chosen for favorable characteristics which maximize the diffusion and adoption of microcomputer technology in the schools. Selection, however, is a relatively poor alternative when considering the comprehensive role of teachers who work with handicapped pupils. There is little evidence that a predisposition to utilize technology will also correlate with other important functions of the teaching role. Further, it appears discriminatory and elitist to rely solely on such variables prior to exerting efforts to train personnel toward acquiring appropriate teaching skills. Given socio-economic influences on opportunities for formative experiences with technology, given the well documented sex-linked biases in the differential socialization processes of males and females in our society, it does not appear appropriate or advisable to rely on selection as the principal means for assuring effective teacher characteristics for successful implementation of technological innovations in special education. Instead, trained personnel who possess both a strong set of skills and knowledge about special education *and* who have also acquired the competencies necessary for successfully integrating microcomputers into the school curriculum for handicapped learners need to be cultivated. The three major sources of such training will be discussed in the following sections.

Inservice Training

We choose to discuss the role of inservice training first because, in our view, the most significant formal and informal initiatives to develop teacher competencies in the use of microcomputers occur at this level. National, state, and local education agencies have simply exercised greater leadership in response to the rapid developments and challenges of the technology revolution than have teacher training programs in most of our colleges and universities. We shall allude to possible explanations for this state of affairs subsequently.

Many of the same factors that influence school administrative decisions on the acquisition of microcomputers influence decisions on inservice teacher training. The first of these are state and federal policies which frequently establish categorical funding opportunities, reimbursement incentives, and less direct forms of educational leadership relative to the diffusion and adoption of technological innovations.

Pressure for innovation from parent and teacher groups provides an additional impetus for shaping the school's response. Teachers who are knowledgeable about microcomputers or who are personally involved with computing activities are often influential in bringing microcomputers to the schools and in motivating others to acquire training.

The private sector also influences policy vis-à-vis philanthropy, political action, and salesmanship. Apple Computer Corporation, for example, achieved favorable state tax advantages through the donation and distribution of a microcomputer to each school in California. This massive contribution to the schools has had a profound impact on the creation of an extended market for Apple products, stimulated an immediate need for inservice training of personnel, and assured exposure of school faculties to at least one type of microcomputer configuration.

A review of the published general education literature indicates a burgeoning effort to increase computer literacy of school personnel through formal inservice training programs (Winner, 1983; DeMark, 1983; Olds, 1983; Nordman, 1982; Furlong, 1983; Gojak, 1983; Johnson, 1981; Burke & Kaiser, 1982; Burke, 1982; Vannatta, 1981; Roberts, 1981). For the most part, inservice approaches to attaining computer literacy for personnel have focused on traditional training vehicles. The "workshop" appears to be the most prevalent form of instruction, augmented by some "hands-on" experiences. Sheingold et al. (1983) described three forms of inservice training following an extensive survey of elementary and secondary schools. The first formal model was the provision of short-term courses or workshops to selected or interested teachers. Training under this paradigm was typically provided by a computer specialist from the district or a local teacher with computer application skills. Administrative support at the school or district level was identified as a critical factor in the provision of such training. Administrative support can impact inservice training in two ways: (1) administrators help determine policies on the acquisition of external resources (e.g., hardware and microcomputer trainers), and (2) they control internal incentives for training, (e.g., the provision of release time for training and practice). This analysis argues for the training of administrators in the factors necessary for effective microcomputer use and training *prior* to providing inservice training for other on-site-school personnel. The remaining two models described by Sheingold et al. involved informal training and networking among inservice teachers and knowledgeable others.

Informal Community Networks and Self-initiated Training

Becker (1983) found the current use pattern to be one in which half of the schools with microcomputers have only one or two teachers regularly using the technology, while the other half of microcomputer using schools have more than two regular users. Selection criteria for teachers who are trained have not been studied. The "grassroots" nature of the microcomputer movement suggests that many of these individuals may be self-selected.

The Sheingold et al. study (1983) found that informal training sessions between computer experts and novice teachers were evident in all districts surveyed. In some districts, enthusiastic teachers who were considered "computer buffs" were observed offering consultation. Informal training tended to take place at mutually agreeable times and did not involve additional compensation. The presence of such highly committed "computer buffs" and opportunities to meet with them was reported to be highly significant in the acceptance of the technology.

A second informal training format described by Sheingold et al. involved the informal tutoring of teachers by knowledgeable students in the school. These student consultants worked collegially with their teachers on computer related activities and generated instructional software subsequently used in classroom instruction.

The use of microcomputers in the schools is an instance of the broader technology revolution in the community at large. The need to acquire computer literacy skills, and the myriad potential applications of computers to virtually all endeavors in our society, has spawned new and heterogeneous groups whose members are bound only by the desire to achieve mastery of the new technology. The form and function of these relatively new community-based "Users Groups" suggest valuable resources for the training of personnel who work with the handicapped in the schools. User groups are characterized by members who come from varied walks of life, age ranges, educational levels, and social and professional strata. The groups are usually organized around a physical locus housing a commercial hardware/software establishment. They meet regularly but are not necessarily attended by the same members at each meeting. Hence, such groups are loosely coupled structures which serve as a support system for their members. Group leadership is not usually defined formally and is more often than not determined simply by the level of competency of its members. The sharing of expertise and a disregard for extraneous status criteria (e.g., age, level of formal education, social class, professional identity) result in such informal user groups realizing an effective means for supporting members seeking to master the new technology.

The community-based user group model is a most promising approach to training large numbers of teachers to acquire appropriate levels of computer literacy for pragmatic application in special education programs. While attendance cannot be prescribed, and training must be self-initiated, support by experts willing to share and model their knowledge and skills with novices, must be available. Such a model permits parents, teachers, students, and other members of the community to interactively work toward reaching commonly held objectives. Such a model demands a close liaison between business, the community, and the schools.

Within the school itself, the presence of a "microcomputer-using teacher" or a microcomputer expert teacher (Becker, 1983), is a widely recognized phenomenon. The role of the computer expert teacher as the nucleus of an informal, school-based network is fundamental in the development of informal training support and opportunities similar to that provided by community-based user groups. The potential of such informal user groups and teacher networks goes beyond development of microcomputer skills, to fostering enthusiasm and opportunity for professional renewal and for encouraging teacher collegiality and professional leadership. While administrative support will be necessary for fostering these teacher directed efforts, it is most important that such support does not inhibit the informal and teacher-initiated nature of the group or network.

Preservice Training

College and university special education preservice training programs have been relatively slow to develop comprehensive programs designed to meet the challenge of microcomputers in the schools. While several general education training programs are currently addressing the issue (e.g., Lockard, 1980; Sherwood, Connor, & Goldberg, 1981; Uhlig, 1982), there is little evidence that such efforts are typical of preservice training of special educators. Uhlig's (1982) survey of teacher training institutions in the Southeastern United States indicated that most schools have a high level of awareness of the developing technology but few have evolved comprehensive, effective responses to this challenge. Several explanations for the relatively slow growth appear plausible. First and foremost, we believe that only a small proportion of college and university faculties in special education are equipped to furnish leadership in technology. Perhaps no more than two percent of the professors responsible for teacher training have had sufficient formal or self-initiated training in technology to prepare them for conceptual and instrumental leadership. Doctoral training in special education only rarely demands competencies in technology; inservice opportunities are limited within most institutions since computer applications at colleges and universities are usually focused on research and analytical capabilities of such technology. The locus of most computer related activities usually occurs in units other than schools of education. Further, acquisition of hardware and software is usually very difficult for training programs within professional schools.

Probably of equal validity is the contention that training faculties are so removed from the schools that they are not fully cognizant of the impact that technology is having on the schools. The evidence strongly suggests that the community and the schools are at the cutting edge of educational applications of technology—with preservice teacher training programs seriously lagging behind. The speed with which technology is being diffused in the school and community may be a particularly potent explanation for why colleges and university programs have been unable to "keep up," let alone offer significant "leadership."

Given the relatively greater availability of microcomputer resources in community schools, and given the greater numbers of school based personnel with demonstrable computer literacy skills, there appears to be good reason for fostering closer collaborative preservice training programs between institutions of higher learning and the schools. If doctoral training programs are not, will not, or cannot provide the trained leadership personnel necessary to developing strong preservice training programs in special education, then preservice teacher training programs have no choice but to look to the community schools for help.

Even if preservice programs were endowed with trained personnel, several pertinent questions remain in offering "appropriate" training to aspiring special education personnel. What will constitute an operational definition of "computer literacy" for special educators? How extensive must such training be to assure pragmatic applications of technology by personnel who work in special education contexts? Is it sufficient to train future special educators to use "off the shelf" software and courseware, or must they master authoring languages, or be proficient in all facets of hardware and software applications? How should such programs be offered? Should they be considered integral to the special education preservice training program, or must they be "concentrations" offered by technology specialists in other departments or units of the institution? These are pressing issues for which the field has no clear empirically based answers. In the remaining sections of this discussion, we will attempt to address some of the more important issues implied by these questions. The analysis centers around our current biases relative to the needs of teachers and the realities of their roles in working with mildly handicapped children in the schools.

TEACHER EFFECTIVENESS AND EFFECTIVE MICROCOMPUTER INSTRUCTION: CONSIDERATIONS FOR TEACHER TRAINING

The past ten years of research in teacher effectiveness has seen a synthesis of findings on variables and conditions related to pupil achievement (Brophy & Evertson, 1977; Stallings, 1980; Good, 1983). While it is outside the scope of this paper to summarize all the variables that are potentially important in the design of training, programs have been developed which incorporate the major effectiveness findings into practical training applications (Stallings, 1977; Englert, 1983). Englert, for example, selected four variables related to teacher effectiveness as measured by student academic achievement. These variables were: (1) high levels of corrective feedback, (2) the number of response opportunities, (3) high levels of academic engaged time, and (4) appropriate performance criteria as measured by task difficulty. These same variables may serve as the basis for the evaluation of microcomputer instruction within the context of the total instructional environment.

Empirically validated variables of teacher effectiveness related to pupil achievement constitute the major criteria for the design of competency based teacher training (Semmel & Semmel, 1976). Because the microcomputer is an instructional medium, the effectiveness criteria are as central to the design of microcomputer teacher training as they are to the design of teacher training in general. Since the innovation is so new, there is not yet an empirical literature upon which to draw. There is little reason to expect, however, that subsequent research will yield any data or identify effectiveness variables that are inconsistent with those related to teacher effectiveness. At the present time, therefore, a reasonable point of departure for the development of microcomputer training programs for teachers must be those variables and conditions that have some empirical support and validation for promoting pupil achievement in the classroom. A related, but no less important reason for conceptualizing microcomputer training as a facet of the total design of a teacher training program, is that microcomputer literacy skills are only a means to an end and that the use of microcomputers must be taught within the context of a broad range of teacher skills in instructional selection, design, modification, planning and individualization, among others.

Software, no matter how well designed, cannot substitute for effective teacher-directed instructional activities. Rather, the role and effectiveness of microcomputer instruction within the child's daily activity is established by the teacher. Assuming basic computer literacy, the teacher still has many key decisions to make regarding the instructional use of microcomputers (e.g., establishing the appropriate level of task difficulty, and assuring congruence with other materials and correlation with the curriculum). In addition to basic mastery over hardware and software, teachers must become adept at software evaluation and selection of software that can, if necessary, be modified. Modifying software to meet individualized pupil needs may be a built-in operation in some programs or may require high level programming skills. Unfortunately, such instructional decisions may be made as much on the basis of the teacher's level of computer skill as on instructional need. The teacher's participation in these decisions is as crucial to the determination of microcomputer effects as is the design of the software itself.

It is our working assumption that effectiveness of microcomputers in the education of mildly handicapped pupils will be a direct function of the effectiveness of the teacher who uses the innovation. There is no reason to believe that the power of the technology will be realized, independent of the teacher's instructional effectiveness without the microcomputer.

Teacher Attitudes

A necessary but not sufficient aspect of any training program is the matter of teacher attitudes toward microcomputers as a classroom tool. Teacher attitudes regarding the educational value of microcomputer technology have been mixed at best. For example, Lichtman (1979) reported that 64% of a sample of inservice and preservice teachers thought computers would improve education. Fifty percent of the sample, however, felt that computers were dehumanizing, and only 30% thought that computers could help them become better teachers. Alderman and Mahler (1977) found that the majority of the faculty of six community colleges where computers were used for instruction felt computers were useful for remedial and low level coursework. However, few believed that computers had the potential to be more effective than other methods of instruction. The basis for these perceptions is unclear. To ensure full utilization of this new technology, training must address these fears while increasing computer literacy in the "broad" sense, i.e., by increasing teachers' understanding of how to use microcomputers effectively.

If we assume that a teacher's overall effectiveness in the classroom sets the boundaries on the effectiveness of microcomputer instruction in that classroom, our goals become twofold: (1) to increase the teacher's overall effectiveness and (2) to help teachers integrate successful classroom behaviors into their microcomputer instruction. Inconsistencies between the teacher's level of instructional effectiveness and that of the microcomputer can have two effects: (1) the microeducational environment (MEE) sets the lower limit to teacher effectiveness (i.e., it is less effective than the teacher in enhancing classroom performance), or (2) the MEE sets an upper limit to classroom effectiveness, providing a less effective teacher with an area of classroom effectiveness.

In the first instance, the MEE cannot provide as successful an academic experience for the student as an effective teacher. These limits are most likely where effective teachers are untrained in manipulating software and unable to utilize the microcomputer to match material to student needs. This suggests the importance of evaluating microcomputer use within the classroom context, and questions the value of microcomputer instruction without active teacher participation.

The second instance, where microcomputer instruction exceeds the effectiveness of other forms of classroom instruction, is expected where the teacher does not provide the same level of effective instructional behaviors as that designed into the software. The benefits of direct microcomputer instruction for mildly handicapped pupils, without teacher participation, are unclear. However, the literature on effective instruction suggests a need for direction from an educator or knowledgeable peer.

We would conclude that there will be a need for a *high* level of teacher involvement in order for pupils to benefit from microcomputer instruction. Despite the promise of high gains in relation to truly individualized and matched instruction, the cost for implementation in terms of time and training is prohibitive. There are pragmatic solutions to this problem offered below; these solutions focus on alternative models for teacher training, including the creation of a new breed of special educators trained in the new technologies while still well grounded in the basics of special education and instructional planning.

RECOMMENDATIONS FOR TEACHER TRAINING: A TWO-TIERED APPROACH

Our assessment of the possibilities for utilization of microcomputers in special education leads to several conclusions: (1) that microcomputer instruction has the potential for directly addressing the mandates of PL 94-142 by providing students with individualized instruction "matched" to their needs, and (2) that the microcomputer's capabilities present new instructional and curriculum options for cognitive and linguistic growth in mildly handicapped pupils. To provide both individualized and innovative instruction, special educators will need training that goes beyond elementary computer literacy.

Although Hofmeister and Thorkildsen (1981) suggested that anticipated advances in software development will eventually diminish the need for teachers to develop advanced computer skills, we feel that such skills will always be necessary in order for instruction to be individualized with precision. It is unlikely that sufficient software/courseware will be available to special educators in the near term. Commercial vendors define special education as a "thin market" and do not invest heavily in programs with such limited potential for profit (see Nordman, 1982).

This contention notwithstanding, the key to maximizing microcomputer technology for handicapped learners is to meld our knowledge of microcomputers with our knowledge of handicapped learners and special education principles. This interactive process cannot be realized by a generalist microcomputer programmer. It requires a special educator who is capable of translating skills and knowledge about technology and special education into effective programs for the handicapped. Without the necessary depth of training, special education personnel will be dependent on "off the shelf" software primarily designed for the regular education market. The situation is analogous to the condition that existed prior to the development of specialized print materials for exceptional pupils—the field was dependent on inappropriate texts—and teachers were and still are required to possess the necessary skills to modify text to meet the needs of their students.

For reasons discussed earlier in the paper, it is our contention that to provide effective microcomputer instruction teachers must have a high level of expertise in both educational and microcomputer technology. While this suggests the need for intensive teacher training in both areas, training programs do not fully resolve the instructional problems of implementing microcomputers in special education programs. A major obstacle to implementation relates to time required for both training and the time required to program and modify instruction to meet individual needs.

If the current special education system has embedded in it constraints which prevent the realization of individualized microcomputer instruction, a new model for special education services may be required. We propose a 'two-tiered' model for the delivery of special education services and for special education teacher training. Both 'tiers' in this model assume comprehensive teacher training in instructional theory and practice. Given this base, teachers in each tier are defined in terms of their level of technological training and expertise, and their role in the instructional system. Educators trained to the 'tier one' level function as special educators within a classroom, and have sufficient computer literacy to use programmed instructional packages with their students. Educators who opt for additional training in microcomputer technology become tier two specialists who function to convert educational practice into software and courseware for individual students.

The model we propose is similar in intent to that of the resource specialist or consultant teacher model. The specialist teacher, whose expertise can be utilized for all children in need of special programming, will provide direct consulting and programming services. The new resource person we propose has a unique role, however, by virtue of combined training in the areas of special education and microcomputer technology. The specialist would have the expertise to build instructional programs around the educational needs of handicapped students. In this way, 'tier one' special education teachers are freed from instructional programming and able to spend more time in direct instruction, while 'tier two' specialists provide individualized programming. While this role differentiation is seen as crucial to the successful application of microcomputer instruction, it puts the burden on teacher trainers to provide opportunities for training at each level of competency. Training opportunities must be provided at both the preservice and inservice levels.

At the inservice level, the informal networking of teachers and others through community- and school-based user groups has some obvious advantages. However, as such informal groups become institutionalized within and beyond the schools, we can expect a widening social-professional gap between those who have embraced the technology revolution and those who have not. The ramifications of such a widening may well be reflected among pupils in our schools as well. Unless we can find effective methods for offering all members of our society an equal opportunity and access to computer literacy skills, we may well realize a society in which technology has *increased* human variance in learning, knowledge, and skills.

Teachers of the handicapped have a particular responsibility to gain mastery over the technology, given the limitations of their students in developing computer skills without assistance. Thus, teacher failures to conquer the technology could directly curtail student access to microcomputers, thus widening the gap between mildly handicapped students and their nonhandicapped peers.

The challenge presented to the schools is how to arrange inservice microcomputer training environments toward maximizing teacher skill acquisition. The schools have become accustomed to the use of relatively ritualistic and generally ineffective formats for training teachers. What is needed are carefully devised opportunities for the development and maintenance of informal professional "user groups" within the schools. There is a need to reallocate time and resources so as to assure sufficient "hands on" experimentation by teachers during and following school hours. Further, there is a need for programs to focus teachers on the importance of integrating software into the framework of the total instructional program.

While we have stressed the primacy of teacher effectiveness, and implicitly the design of microeducational environments (MEEs) as indicated by the integration of microcomputer instruction into the curriculum and program planning process, there are a number of unique and distinctive features of microcomputer instruction which suggest additional training needs. There is a need to learn to utilize the instructional capabilities which are *unique* to microcomputer technology. These capabilities include word processing programs, which provide new modes of instruction and opportunities for cognitive and written language development, and the development of programming languages such as Logo and Delta Drawing. These developments are truly new in the sense that they are unique to the programming and word processing capabilities of the microcomputer. While much research and development is needed in this area, their potential must not be overlooked. It would indeed be unfortunate if training programs provide teachers basic computer literacy, only to have the new skills applied to the equivalent of electronic work books.

Preservice institutions for teacher training have similar challenges to meet. If, as we believe to be the case, few teacher trainers themselves have the skills necessary to prepare others to utilize the new technology, the need to develop an initial leadership base is paramount. One option, discussed earlier, is to exploit this opportunity to develop closer collaborative relationships between the schools and teacher training institutions. The utilization of teacher microcomputer 'experts' in teacher training programs would help to direct this new training in effective and pragmatic directions.

In effect, we take the position that the advent of microcomputer technology offers special education a significant challenge: We have at our disposal a potentially powerful medium for significantly enhancing the education of handicapped pupils, but it will be necessary to train special education personnel to become proficient in the knowledge and skills needed to maximize its applications. We propose, too, that significant changes in training and the delivery of service will be necessary for the effective application of this technology to special education. We have been presented with a new technology, the mastery of which may well be viewed as one of the salient defining features of what makes a special educator "Special."

REFERENCES

Becker, H. J. (1983). *School uses of microcomputers*. Baltimore: Johns Hopkins U., Center for Social Organization of Schools.

Brophy J. E., & Evertson, C. M. (1977). Teacher behavior and student learning. In G. D. Borich (Ed.), *The appraisal of teaching*. Reading, MA: Addison-Wesley.

Burke, L. (1982). Getting to know your computer. *Classroom Computer News, 2*(5), 4-42.

Burke, M., & Kaiser, J. (1982). Who took a Byte from my Apple Rom. *NASSP Bulletin, 66*(455), 83-86.

DeMark, P. (1983). Getting started and staying on track. *Classroom Computer News, 3*(6), 58-59.

Englert, C. (1983). Measuring special education teachers' effectiveness. *Exceptional Children, 50*(2), 247-255.

Furlong, M. (1983). Introducing microcomputers into the social studies classroom. *Social Studies Review, 22*(2), 61-65.

Gojak, L. (1983). Taking the first step with a computer. *Arithmetic Teacher, 30*(7), 34-40.

Good, T. L. (1983). Classroom research: A decade of progress, *Educational Psychologist, 18*(3), 127-144.

Hofmeister, A. M., & Thorkildsen, R. J. (1981). Videodisc technology and the preparation of special education teachers. *Teacher Education and Special Education, 4*(3), 34-39.

Lockard, J. (1980). Computers blossom at a small school in Iowa. *Instructional Innovator, 25*(6), 25.

Nordman, R. (1982). An effective microcomputer inservice: Designing and using awareness workshops. *ERIC Document,* ED229352.

Olds, Henry. (1983). Teaching the teachers. *Classroom Computer News, 3*(6), 52-55.

Papert, S. (1980). *Mindstorms: Children, computers and powerful ideas*. New York: Basic Books.

Roberts, H. (1981). Linking computer to curriculum starts with the teacher. *Educational Computer Magazine, 1*(1), 27-28.

Rosenshine, B. V. (1979). Content, time and direct instruction. In J. Peterson & H. Walberg (Eds.), *Research on teaching*. Berkeley: McCutchan.

Semmel, M. I., Semmel, D. S., Cosden, M. A., Gerber, M., & Goldman, S. (1983). An analysis and development of naturalistic and experimentally constructed microeducational environments for mildly handicapped learners. Santa Barbara: UCSB, Graduate School of Education.

Semmel, M. I., & Semmel, D. S. (1976). Competency based teacher education: An overview. *Behavioral Disorders, 1*(2), 68-89.

Semmel, M. I., Gottlieb, J., & Robinson, N. (1979). Mainstreaming: Perspectives on educating handicapped children in the public school. In E. Berliner (Ed.), *Review of research in education.* American Educational Research Assoc.

Sheingold, K., Kane, J. H., & Endereweit, M. E. (1983). Microcoputer use in schools: Developing a research agenda. *Harvard Educational Review, 53*(4), 412-432.

Sherwood, R., Connor, J., & Goldberg, K. (1981). Developing computer literacy and competency for preservice and inservice teachers. *Journal of Computers in Mathematics and Science Teaching, 1*(2), 23-24.

Stallings, J. (1980). Allocated academic learning time revisited, or beyond time on task. *Educational Researcher, 9*(11), 11-16.

Uhlig, G. (1982). Microcomputer literacy and teacher education in the Southeastern United States. *ERIC Document,* ED 226721.

Vannatta, G. (1981). Computers for instructional purposes—a case study. *Viewpoints in Teaching and Learning, 52*(2), 37-45.

Winner, A. (1983). Computer literacy in the elementary school. *AEDS Journal, 16*(3), 153-165.

Evaluating Microcomputer Programs

Randy Elliot Bennett

ABSTRACT. Much interest is being expressed in schools across the nation about the use of microcomputers to improve the delivery of special and regular education services. With this interest has come the need to evaluate educational programs utilizing microcomputers so that decisions about program improvement and expansion can be made. This paper discusses the evaluation of special education programs that incorporate microcomputers as a major instructional tool.

Microcomputers are currently being used in a variety of ways to improve the delivery of special education services. Computers are being employed to keep pupil record information, score psychological tests, teach basic skills, synthesize speech for those students who cannot speak, and help update the job competencies of staff members (Bennett, 1982).

For many, the use of the microcomputer as a teaching tool is especially attractive. For one, the microcomputer's capacity to respond differently depending upon the actions of the learner offers the potential for more fully individualizing the presentation of instruction (Bennett, 1982). Second, the machine's ability to keep track of student responses gives a simple, but accurate, means of measuring pupil progress.

Though the potential benefits of using microcomputers in the classroom appear substantial, there are several reasons why special services personnel should approach the incorporation of microcomputers with caution (Bennett, 1984). Primary among these reasons is the high cost of such programs. Hardware and software need to be purchased and a substantial investment in staff training often needs to be made if personnel are to make effective use of this new technology.

Requests for reprints should be sent to: Randy Elliot Bennett, Division of Measurement Research and Services, Educational Testing Service, Princeton, New Jersey 08541.

© 1984 by The Haworth Press, Inc. All rights reserved.

In addition to cost, there are little hard data supporting the effectiveness of microcomputers as a teaching tool. While the technology seems exciting and the potential benefits appear substantial, traditional methods may prove as effective.

For these reasons it makes good sense for special educators to carefully evaluate programs incorporating microcomputers. The results of such evaluation can offer guidance as to how programs can be improved and whether they should be expanded to other schools in the district, other grades, or other populations. This paper suggests three areas to consider in conducting such evaluations.

REVIEW THE PROGRAM'S DESIGN

All programs should be based upon an explicit plan that details what conditions are necessary to run the program and how the program will be carried out. A written program design helps guide staff in carrying out the program and offers specifications against which the operation of the program can later be evaluated.

For example, a design for a microcomputer-based reading resource room program should identify the general goals of the program (e.g., to improve basic reading skills), the characteristics of those who will receive the program (e.g., learning disabled students with IEP goals focusing on basic reading skill development), the software and hardware that will be used (e.g., 5 IBM Personal Computers and the *Writing to Read* series, [Martin, 1982]), the staff needed to operate the program (e.g., one certified resource teacher trained in the use of the IBM Personal Computer), and how the program will be evaluated.

In evaluating the written program design, several factors should be considered (Maher & Bennett, 1984). First, the design should be reviewed to make sure that it clearly presents all the information necessary for staff to effectively implement the program. Next, the compatibility of the program with district capabilities should be assessed. If the design calls for the purchase of five microcomputers, attempts should be made to verify that district resources will permit not only the acquisition, but repair of the machines when they break down and the purchase of needed supplies (e.g., diskettes, printer ribbons, paper).

Third, the internal consistency of the various elements of the program should be considered. If the primary goal of the microcomputer-based reading resource room program is to facilitate basic decoding skills, the software slated for use should emphasize reading and not unrelated topics such as learning to use the computer's color graphics capabilities.

Finally, the extent to which the program is theoretically sound should be determined. Goals and activities should reflect the dictates of good professional practice. Controversial treatments, such as the perceptual-motor stratagems once used to teach reading, should raise flags for program reviewers.

In considering theoretical soundness, the quality of instructional materials should also be reviewed. Of particular importance is the quality of the educational software that will form the basis of the program. Several characteristics make for quality in software. Among these characteristics are educational value, accuracy, values orientation, attractiveness, and friendliness.

The educational value of software refers in part to the match between the software and the goals of the microcomputer program, a consideration previously treated under internal consistency. In addition, the extent to which psychological principles are incorporated into the software is an important facet of educational value. For example, reinforcement should be provided for correct responses and not for incorrect ones. Programs such as *Hangman* (a word guessing game) are notorious for encouraging children to respond incorrectly because the reinforcement for the wrong response (i.e., seeing the stick figure hang) is more powerful than that for the correct response.

Accuracy denotes the degree to which the world is correctly portrayed. Statements in social studies, science, and other programs should be factually accurate. English punctuation, spelling, and grammar should be correct. Finally, minorities and females should be properly represented; racial and sex stereotypes should be absent.

In addition to educational value and accuracy, the match between the values implied by the software and those of the school and community should be assessed. Some software products, such as the *Alien Addition* program from the *Arcademic Skill Builders in Math* series (Chaffin & Maxwell, 1982), require students to destroy alien space ships as part of a mathematics drill and practice exercise. The violence inherent in such programs may prove objectionable to some parents and school staff members.

The attractiveness of educational software refers to the extent to which the package takes advantage of the unique capabilities of the computer. These capabilities include sound, graphics, color, and branching (the ability of the computer to respond differently based on the input of the pupil). Though violent, programs such as *Alien Addition* use arcade-game sound, color, and graphics, which are proven quantities in attracting and holding the attention of children.

Last, the "friendliness" of software should be considered. Friendliness is a term commonly used to mean ease of use. Software should provide clear directions to the pupil with respect to the task to be performed. Incorrect responses, no matter how illogical, should be handled smoothly, without the program inexplicably ceasing to operate. Display screens should be arranged so that text is easy to read.

In sum, the major objective of design review is to make sure that there is a meaningful plan for carrying out the microcomputer program. Without careful planning, few programs utilizing new technology will be likely to succeed.

REVIEW THE PROGRAM'S OPERATION

In addition to reviewing the design of a microcomputer program, it is useful to assess the program's implementation. Implementation evaluation should focus on the extent to which the program is being operated as stated in the program design.

In the case of the microcomputer-based reading resource room program mentioned above, several factors should be considered. A fundamental question is whether all hardware and software have arrived and are in working order. Clearly, the goals of the reading program cannot be achieved if most machines are inoperable and the proper instructional software has not been received. Also of importance is the extent to which the program is reaching its target population. If attendance is poor, program goals will not be achieved either. Finally, the types of activities actually engaged in by pupils should be checked to insure that students are working toward improving their reading skills and not simply playing computer games.

The major focus of implementation evaluation should be to determine the extent to which the microcomputer program is operating in concert with the specifications contained in the program design. Discrepancies between actual operation and design plans may or may not represent problem situations; teachers may discover that students quickly tire of the instructional software and that some amount of instruction in generating computer graphics interests pupils and provides additional reading practice. Discrepancies should, therefore, be evaluated to determine if the program's operation should be changed or if the discrepancy instead represents a useful innovation that should be permanently incorporated into program plans.

REVIEW THE PROGRAM'S OUTCOMES

The outcomes or impact of a microcomputer-based program can be thought to include considerations of goal attainment, cause-effect relations, unintended effects, cost-effectiveness, consumer reaction, and program change. Each of these considerations deserves some discussion.

When most educators speak of evaluation they are referring to goal attainment; that is, the extent to which a program has achieved what it set out to accomplish. Measuring the goal attainment of a microcomputer program typically involves taking independent measures of pupil achievement and comparing the results with program goals. For a microcomputer-based program designed to increase students' rapid recall of basic number facts, the average number of problems correctly completed by students on a flash card exercise might be used as one measure of program goal attainment. An average recall score that matched or exceeded the target set at the beginning of the program would provide the first major piece of evidence to support the program's effectiveness in attaining its goals.

Though evaluation data may suggest that goals have been achieved, it is presumptuous to assume that the microcomputer program is necessarily responsible for this accomplishment. Many unrelated influences can result in goal attainment or the appearance of goal attainment (Campbell & Stanley, 1963). For example, because of their learning difficulties, many children in the microcomputer math program might also be receiving home tutoring focusing on improving recall of basic facts. It is possible that this home tutoring program is more responsible for the students' improvement than the microcomputer program.

The methods needed to definitively rule out the influence of other factors on goal attainment are rarely practical in special education settings. For example, the random assignment of pupils to treatments violates both legal and ethical principles that state that students must be assigned to programs based on educational need and not on the dictates of evaluation design. The cause-effect relationship between the microcomputer program and the outcomes observed must, therefore, be supported by other means. Cause-effect relations are most commonly supported by attempting to rule out competing explanations for goal attainment. Such possible explanations as other programs, the effects of normal growth and development, and changes in the nature of the group of students participating in the program between inception and outcome assessment should be considered.

In addition to goal attainment and cause-effect relations, a third important consideration in the evaluation of microcomputer outcomes is unintended effects. Unintended, or side, effects are most commonly assessed in the pharmaceutical industry, where a drug may be effective in reducing the patient's blood pressure but at the same time cause long-term liver damage. Microcomputer programs may have any of a wide range of positive or negative side effects. Physically handicapped students may achieve the program's intended goal: "to learn how to program the computer using specialized input devices such as chin switches." At the same time, they may develop more confidence in themselves and a greater sense of self-worth, both beneficial, but probably unintended, effects. On the other hand, the program may induce increased anxiety in teachers, who have not had the time to fully learn the capabilities of the machine who are beginning to feel for the first time that they know less than their rapidly progressing students.

A fourth aspect of outcome assessment is cost-effectiveness, a topic of growing interest in days of decreasing resources. A microcomputer program to teach the mentally retarded to manage money may achieve its goals, be proven the cause of that goal attainment, and, in addition, have unintended positive effects on self-concept. However, even with these positive outcomes, there may be a less expensive way to achieve the same results.

As with cause-effect relations, definitive conclusions about cost-effectiveness are difficult to obtain in educational settings (Maher & Bennett, 1984). Hence, judgments of cost-effectiveness are best made tentatively.

To develop a rough appreciation for the cost-effectiveness of a microcomputer program another program designed to achieve the same goals must be found. Students in the comparison program must be at the same initial skill level in the goal area as those in the microcomputer program. In addition, they must be similar on other relevant learning characteristics (e.g., cognitive ability). Finally, the comparison program must use a different means to achieve the goals common to both programs (e.g., traditional work sheet instruction instead of microcomputers). Otherwise, the microcomputer program will, in essence, be compared to itself and the results will prove meaningless for judgments of cost-effectiveness. After both programs have been allowed to operate for some time, program costs and goal attainment levels can be compared. The program that appears to produce the greater goal attainment for the lesser cost can be tentatively judged the more cost-effective.

Consumer reaction is a fifth consideration in evaluating the outcomes of microcomputer programs. In special education in particular, parents have shown themselves to be a powerful force. Getting the reactions of these consumers to the programs offered their children can be helpful in lending "social validity" (Wolf, 1978) to the effort. In addition, students themselves can often provide useful perceptions about what aspects of the microcomputer program were of greatest value to them.

The final consideration in evaluating the outcomes of a microcomputer program is how the program should be changed. Decisions of program change include expanding the microcomputer learning disability reading resource room program to other high schools in the district, to other populations of students (such as those in Title 1 programs), or downward to the junior high level. Program change also includes such decisions as those to provide more training in the operation of the microcomputers to teachers, to utilize a new microcomputer vendor for future programs because of the reliability of the currently used machine, and to shift to a more promising instructional software package. Decisions of program change should be based on as much information about the program, from design to implementation to outcome, as is available.

CONCLUSION

Microcomputers are being used with increasing frequency to help improve the delivery of special education services. Because microcomputers have the potential to increase the individualization of instruction as well as more efficiently track the progress of exceptional students, microcomputers hold particular promise for instructional purposes.

The development and improvement of special education programs that use microcomputers is largely dependent upon the extent to which decision makers have trustworthy information about program characteristics. Systematic reviews of program design, implementation, and outcomes can help special educators insure that the best uses are made of this potentially powerful educational resource.

REFERENCES

Bennett, R. (1982). Applications of microcomputer technology to special education. *Exceptional Children, 49,* 106-113.

Bennett, R. (1984). Myths and realities in automating special education information management systems. *Journal of Learning Disabilities, 17,* 52-54.

Campbell, D., & Stanley, J. (1963). *Experimental and quasi-experimental designs for research.* Chicago: Rand McNally.

Chaffin, J., & Maxwell, B. (1982). *Arcademic skill builders in math.* Allen, TX: Developmental Learning Materials.

Maher, C., & Bennett, R. (1984). *Planning and evaluating special education services.* Englewood Cliffs, NJ: Prentice-Hall.

Martin, J. (1982). *The teacher's manual for the Writing to Read System.* Boca Raton, FL: IBM.

Wolf, M. (1978). Social validity: The case for subjective measurement *or* How applied behavior analysis is finding its heart. *Journal of Applied Behavior Analysis, 11,* 203-214.

Assessing and Facilitating School Readiness for Microcomputers

Robert J. Illback
Linda Hargan

ABSTRACT. Microcomputers represent a complex educational innovation requiring a planned change approach to program implementation. In this paper, the AVICTORY approach, a framework for assessing organizational readiness for microcomputers, is delineated. A case illustration is presented to demonstrate the relevance of the approach and a strategy for operationalizing and measuring organizational readiness is provided. Activities which may facilitate school readiness for microcomputers are also discussed.

Microcomputers have been hailed as a revolutionary development in education. During the past few years, a dramatic increase in the use of microcomputers for educational applications has occurred. Some general uses of microcomputers include computer-managed instruction, computer-assisted instruction, word processing, information management for administrative purposes, and test scoring and interpretation, among others. Substantial education resources are being spent on hardware and software at the present time, and as the public's awareness of computers and desire for computer literacy increases, the amount of money spent for microcomputer education can only increase.

The growth of microcomputer utilization is particularly noticeable within the special services community. An exciting array of special educational applications has been described, and their potential for positively affecting the delivery of instruction to special needs pupils appears promising (see Taber, 1983, for an overview of these applications).

Requests for reprints should be sent to: Robert J. Illback, Department of Student Services, Ft. Knox Dependent Schools, Ft. Knox, Kentucky 40121.

© 1984 by The Haworth Press, Inc. All rights reserved.

As microcomputers become part of the fabric of American education, and as school districts spend increasing portions of already shrinking budgets on expensive hardware and software, it is important to consider the success of past educational innovations. Education seems particularly susceptible to adopting and then discarding "revolutionary" concepts and innovations. Some prominent examples of this phenomenon include the New Math, open classrooms, and career education, to name but a few. At least some of these educational innovations have had commendable features, but have nonetheless been relegated to the "junk heap," often due to inadequate preparation by schools.

The central thesis of this paper is that for schools to fully determine the applicability of microcomputers to the educational problems of special needs children, a planned change approach to microcomputer implementation must be taken. A critical element of this planned change approach involves the assessment of a range of organizational factors which may be predictive of the effectiveness of a special services microcomputer program. First, the concept of organizational readiness for microcomputer utilization will be delineated. Then, a case illustration which demonstrates the utility of the approach will be provided, followed by a strategy for operationalizing and measuring organizational readiness. Finally, some conclusions about how to facilitate organizational readiness will be discussed.

ORGANIZATIONAL READINESS FOR AN INNOVATION

Microcomputers are a technological innovation and as such can be seen as representative of an emerging body of knowledge available to educators. There is extensive literature which suggests that the relationship between the emergence of new knowledge and its application to social problems is not always clear. For example, a study sponsored by the National Science Foundation (1973) concluded that the average time lag between discovery and systematic use of ten major technical inventions was nearly twenty years and some argue that education is likely to take even longer to fully implement innovations (Miles, 1965).

Much attention has been paid to the problems of knowledge utilization and innovation diffusion in the program evaluation literature (Human Interaction Research Institute, 1976). A distillation of this literature reveals that a major contributing factor to inadequate utilization of innovations is the readiness of host organizations to incorporate the innovation into their routine. "Organizational readiness" can be conceptualized in several ways, but an increasingly popular conception is offered by Davis and Salasin (1975) in the form of the AVICTORY model. AVICTORY is an acronym for eight factors believed predictive of readiness: *A*bility, *V*alues, *I*nformation, *C*ircumstances, *T*iming, *O*bligation, *R*esistance, and *Y*ield.

Ability

The ability of the organization (e.g., school building, district, cooperative) to commit resources is critical to the success or failure of the special services microcomputer project. Perhaps the most critical resource of all is the most overlooked: human resources. A considerable amount of time and effort must be devoted to planning and implementation aspects, such as staff training, decision-making about hardware and software, and discussions about roles and responsibilities. In the absence of clear sanctions for these activities, the project will founder. Additional dimensions include informational resources (e.g., access to the district curriculum guides which should guide software purchases), and financial resources (which typically set the parameters for whatever project is envisioned).

Values

The values of various organizational constituencies also need to be assessed in relation to the special services microcomputer project. These constituencies may include special education teachers, relevant administrators, parents, students, and others. In this regard, it may be important to discern the attitudes of a particular group toward the special services microcomputer project, especially if that group is critical to the project's success. For example, what are the beliefs and attitudes of special education teachers in relation to using microcomputers as a mode of educational service delivery?

Information

This factor focuses on the quality and credibility of the innovation, and the availability of information sufficient to implement it. Those responsible for implementing the special services microcomputer project need to be provided with a context from which to view the innovation in relation to other educational activities, and they need to receive guidance regarding the activities deemed suitable for microcomputer usage. For example, teachers need to be aware of the prevailing organizational philosophy regarding microcomputers (e.g., using the computer to present instruction to students vs. teaching students *about* the computer), and they need curriculum to incorporate various software programs into their classroom routine.

Circumstances

Stable environmental and organizational attributes which influence change also need to be assessed. Innovations are received more readily in situations where roles are already well-defined, program procedures are established, and the quality of interpersonal relationships is enduring. Thus, it may be useful to assess the degree to which the special services programs are currently functioning smoothly in order to determine those characteristics which may facilitate or inhibit the utilization of microcomputers.

Timing

Timing has to do with dynamic environmental and organizational factors which may influence utilization of the innovation. For example, when there is tremendous turmoil within an organization, it is not a good time to introduce a new program (especially one as complex and potentially unnerving as one involving microcomputers). On the other hand, there may be times of low stress for the organization (e.g., summer) when the project could be carefully considered and planned.

Obligation

The felt-need, or obligation, of key persons within the organization to alter current practices by developing their capacity to utilize microcomputers is a critical element in the adoption of new technology. If microcomputers are not seen by potential program staff as facilitating important goals of the instructional program, their adoption may be jeopardized.

Resistance

There are many forms which resistance to an innovation can take, ranging from direct and vocal opposition to the required changes to benign neglect of project activities. The net result is the same: a diminished capacity to fully implement the special services microcomputer program. Prior to the introduction of microcomputers into the service delivery system, it is critical to assess the nature and scope of oppositional factors which can sabotage the best efforts of the project manager.

Yield

Acceptance of an innovation occurs most readily when the incentives for engaging in the new approach are clearly perceived by program participants. Incentives to special services personnel for using microcomputers may include an increased ability to individualize, increased planning time due to more efficient management of pupil progress data, recognition by colleagues for being innovative, and advancement within the organization.

CASE ILLUSTRATION OF ORGANIZATIONAL READINESS FACTORS

A case illustration of how microcomputers were introduced into a special services system can clarify the usefulness of applying a planned change approach. The plan developed by this organization will be described and then an analysis made with regard to each of the factors in the AVICTORY model.

Microcomputers were introduced into the special education programs in a regional special services cooperative in Kentucky in the Fall of 1982. The 10 districts in this cooperative are small, primarily rural establishments with a total enrollment of about 13,000. Approximately 12% of the school population (1560 students) is served in 83 special education units.

Special education teachers were surveyed informally by the director of the cooperative in the late summer of 1982 regarding their interest in using microcomputers in the classrooms. As a result of teachers' high level of interest, plans were developed to obtain sufficient funds over a 2-3 year period to purchase 35-40 microcomputers. This number of computers would allow for at least one per building for the special education programs, or approximately one computer for every 2 teachers. As funds were obtained, the computers would be placed first in the elementary programs, then the middle schools and junior high school programs, and finally into the high schools.

The microcomputers were to be used primarily for computer-assisted instruction (CAI). Initially, the machines were to be allocated to the mildly handicapped programs across all levels; then, the computers were to be integrated into the more severely handicapped programs for CAI, but were also to be used in conjunction with adaptive devices to facilitate instruction.

All special education teachers were given 6-8 hours of training in October and November and the first batch of computers was placed in classrooms in December. The content of the training included familiarity with hardware, introduction to computer literacy, terminology, computer-assisted applications for the mildly handicapped, and guidelines for software selection and review.

The initial plan was to rotate the 10 computers among the 30 elementary teachers so that each class would have access to the machines several months of the year. As it happened, additional funds became available in January, 1983 and again in late summer of 1983, so that by Fall of 1983 the cooperative had obtained 37 microcomputers. There was at least one, and sometimes two, for the special education programs housed in every building, and the cooperative was approaching the "one for every two teachers" mark set as a goal. An additional day of training and opportunity for software review was offered two times in the Spring of 1983. In addition, the cooperative joined the Minnesota Educational Computing Consortium (MECC) in the summer of 1983 so that teachers could gain access to more educational software.

On the surface, the microcomputer project appeared to be moving well ahead of schedule as the program completed its first year of implementation. However, at about this time, indications of problems became apparent. Some of these problems appear to have been the direct result of not sufficiently taking into account critical readiness factors.

Ability

The fiscal ability of the cooperative to purchase needed hardware and software was greater than was originally thought; funds became available in about one-third the anticipated time. Overlooked, however, was the role of the special education teachers themselves in the overall planning and implementation process. Teachers were asked whether they were interested, but from then on many decisions were made by the director of the cooperative and superintendents of the involved districts without consulting teachers. For example, in making decisions about where to initially place computers, insufficient attention was given to the relative ability of specific teachers or programs to fully utilize the machines. As a result, the computers were sometimes used in superficial and mechanical ways (e.g., for rewarding students), and in at least one situation, the computer was ultimately removed. In fact, in those districts in which the first teacher to have the computer was computer competent, sophisticated, and enthusiastic, the interest and knowledge of other teachers in the building grew and appeared to be associated with the success of the program as it developed over time.

Values

While the interest of the special education teachers and superintendents was initially assessed, it appears that the information obtained was not comprehensive enough to be useful in planning the program. For example, it would have been helpful to know more specifically what attitudes special education teachers held about how computers can help instruct special students. Additionally, the failure to determine the beliefs and attitudes of the regular educator responsible for microcomputers in each district resulted in problems, such as disputes about the relative worth of various hardware and software, and concerns about access to and storage of the equipment. Awareness of these attitudes would have helped program planners avoid these problems.

Information

The training offered to the special education teachers prior to their receiving microcomputers was critical and definitely contributed to the initial success of the program. However, an important area of training was not addressed and remains a problem. Teacher training should go beyond criteria for selecting software and focus on how software can be appropriately integrated into the curriculum. Even after the first year of activities, teachers were still changing their curriculum or instructional sequence to incorporate software, rather than fitting software to the curricular structure that already existed. This approach to incorporating microcomputers can result in confusing children who are exposed to skills via CAI that are out of sequence with the instruction delivered in their regular classrooms. Training efforts should initially emphasize the necessity for appropriate curricular integration. The relation of the computer project to the regular program of instruction is vital *information.*

A second problem related to information is that teachers use information differentially and progress at different rates. It was not initially anticipated that some teachers would quickly move ahead on their own. For example, some teachers rapidly developed the skills needed to author their own lessons and to use management software for pupil diagnosis and record keeping. Unfortunately, little planning on how to facilitate the growth of advanced users had been completed so that the progress of this group was left primarily to its own devices.

Circumstances and Timing

The decision-making process for determining when and how to introduce microcomputers appears to have adequately taken account of these factors in that funds were available, people were interested, the idea was timely given the attention to microcomputers in the media, and the host organizations were generally stable and free of disruptive influences.

Obligation

As previously mentioned, insufficient weight was given to the degree of felt-need on the part of some teachers. Since teachers will need to expend a considerable amount of time and effort in planning and implementing the project, obligation appears to have been a critical and highly predictive factor in relation to eventual level of use. In classrooms where the teacher does not feel especially obliged to participate, the prospect for dust-gathering is considerable.

Resistance

Resistance to the microcomputer project itself was exhibited by about 10% of the special education teachers involved. Most often this resistance took the form of benign neglect or passive resistance (e.g., "I'm afraid the students will damage the equipment."). Only rarely was active resistance seen (e.g., "I don't want anything to do with a microcomputer."). It might have been possible to diffuse these concerns had more systematic information about resistance been gathered earlier.

Yield

The vast majority of the teachers in the special services cooperative had no difficulty immediately perceiving the benefits of computer-assisted instruction to their program and hence embraced the concept enthusiastically. Those few who did not perceive the benefits reacted more favorably after some exposure to other teachers who were using the computers and after seeing the time-savings which the machines could create (e.g., by scheduling students into the resource room). Modeling and demonstration can play a significant role in enhancing teacher perceptions of potential payoff.

OPERATIONALIZING ORGANIZATIONAL READINESS

As demonstrated by the case illustration, systematic organizational assessment can play an important role in planning for the introduction of microcomputers. Methods have been developed for use of the AVICTORY framework to assess school readiness for other innovations (Glaser & Backer, 1980; Kiresuk, 1980), and this methodology appears useful for gaining information on the introduction of microcomputers to special education.

Specifically, the AVICTORY framework allows for the construction of a questionnaire composed of items covering the various readiness aspects. For example, a question about *V*alues might inquire into the respondent's beliefs about the role microcomputers can play in the instruction of special needs learners. Similarly, an *I*nformation item could seek to probe the respondent's awareness of microcomputer applications. The design of items and formats should follow standard test development procedures (see Tuckman, 1972, for a comprehensive review of the technical issues involved in this task).

An example of such a scale can be seen in Table 1. Under each of the eight AVICTORY categories are listed specific questions relating to special needs applications of microcomputers. Each item is designed to tap a different aspect of that particular readiness factor in order to provide a well-rounded picture of the dimension.

To obtain a diagnostic profile of the organization, the opinion

Table 1

Organizational Readiness for Microcomputers in Special Services

Directions: Circle the response which most accurately reflects your current thinking about the use of microcomputers <u>with special needs learners</u> (SNL).

Statement	Disagree (1)	Mildly Disagree (2)	Can't Decide (3)	Mildly Agree (4)	Agree (5)
Ability					
I have the necessary training to successfully use microcomputers in my program with SNL.	1	2	3	4	5
I can meet the educational needs of special needs children in my program through computer assisted instruction.	1	2	3	4	5
Overall, I think this building is capable of successfully carrying out a microcomputer project for SNL.	1	2	3	4	5
Overall, I think this school district is capable of successfully carrying out a microcomputer project for SNL.	1	2	3	4	5
Values					
I believe microcomputers can play a valuable role in delivering instruction to SNL.	1	2	3	4	5
I think people in this organization will support the implementation of a microcomputer project for SNL	1	2	3	4	5
This organization has a history of supporting change and innovation for children with learning and behavior problems.	1	2	3	4	5
I believe my immediate supervisor values the use of microcomputers in the classroom with special needs children.	1	2	3	4	5
Information					
I am aware of instructional software which is available and appropiate for use in my program with SNL	1	2	3	4	5
I know how to obtain assistance in implementing a microcomputer program for SNL	1	2	3	4	5
I know how to obtain further training in microcomputer applications that are relevant to me.	1	2	3	4	5

Table 1 (continued)

Circumstances

Technical assistance in using microcomputers is available to me should I need it.	1	2	3	4	5
I have adequate time during the week to plan for the use of microcomputers with SNL.	1	2	3	4	5
My participation in the microcomputer program will be supported by my colleagues.	1	2	3	4	5
There are sufficient resources available to me to insure my success in using microcomputers with SNL.	1	2	3	4	5
Other factors exist in my situation which will make it difficult for me to fully participate in a microcomputer program.	5	4	3	2	1
My participation in a microcomputer program will be supported by my immediate supervisor.	1	2	3	4	5

Timing

There are circumstances occurring in the organization right now which will negatively affect the implementation of the microcomputer program.	5	4	3	2	1
Microcomputers can be introduced into my program at the present time without any difficulty.	1	2	3	4	5

Obligation

I am interested in improving my skills in utilizing the microcomputer for instruction of SNL.	1	2	3	4	5
I am willing to change some of my instructional methods and materials to accommodate the use of the microcomputer.	1	2	3	4	5
Microcomputer assisted instruction will benefit the SNL in my program.	1	2	3	4	5
I am willing to spend the extra time needed to use microcomputers in my program.	1	2	3	4	5
I am willing to work with other staff members and consultants to become more effective in using the microcomputer.	1	2	3	4	5
In general, I think there is a felt need in my building to expand and improve microcomputer utilization for SNL.	1	2	3	4	5

Table 1 (continued)

In general, I think there is a felt need in this school district to expand and improve microcomputer utilization for SNL.	1	2	3	4	5

Resistance

Gearing up to use microcomputers will take too much time away from my regular program of instruction	5	4	3	2	1
I am not qualified to use microcomputers in delivering instruction to SNL, and should not have to.	5	4	3	2	1
Due to constraints imposed by the curriculum, I cannot modify my instructional program to incorporate microcomputer assisted instruction.	5	4	3	2	1
Due to the organization and management of my program, computer assisted instruction will be difficult to implement.	5	4	3	2	1
I do not believe that microcomputers will have a dramatic impact on education, and therefore they do not warrant my involvement and effort.	5	4	3	2	1

Yield

Microcomputer usage will give me an opportunity to learn new skills which will allow me to be more effective.	1	2	3	4	5
I am likely to get positive recognition for using microcomputers in my program.	1	2	3	4	5
Microcomputers will benefit the students in my program.	1	2	3	4	5
Microcomputers are a cost-efficient method for delivering instructional services.	1	2	3	4	5

statements are rated by a representative sample of organization members on a five-point Likert scale. It is then possible to aggregate the data by question, by category, by subgroup, or for the total sample in order to draw inferences about the facilitating and inhibiting factors. An example of such an aggregate profile is seen in Table 2.

The effectiveness and appropriateness of this strategy for a particular school should be determined in relation to a range of psychometric, ethical, and practical considerations. In adopting this approach, the practitioner is encouraged to follow accepted practices of scale development and validation (American Psychological Association, 1974) and to cautiously interpret data gleaned from this process. Additionally, ethical concerns, such as the professional's responsibility to ensure that data collected during the organizational assessment are appropriately used, should be considered. Finally, in some situations it may not be feasible or relevant to engage in this degree of systematic planning, and a more informal approach might be appropriate. In any case, it should be recognized that what has been described is a way of thinking about program planning and implementation, and not a prescription for success appropriate in

Table 2

AVICTORY Organizational Profile

		Mean Rating			
1	2	3	4	5	
			X		ABILITY
			X		VALUES
	X				INFORMATION
			X		CIRCUMSTANCES
		X			TIMING
		X			OBLIGATION
		X			RESISTANCE
	X				YIELD

every context. Local circumstances should dictate how this particular management tool is utilized.

CONCLUSION

Before initiating a microcomputer project for special services programs, we believe it is extremely important to carefully consider the philosophy, goals, principles, and procedures for the project, and to attempt to reach consensus about these with staff and other participants (including students). There are several essential decisions which need to be reached in this process (e.g., Will the focus be on learning from the computer or on learning about it?). To the degree staff are involved early in making these decisions, their eventual level of participation and understanding will be enhanced. We also believe there is a need for a "marketing" strategy when introducing an innovation of this complexity into an already complicated organization. Thus, it may be useful to form a committee of key persons within the school, provide them with essential information, and guide their efforts in transmitting this information to colleagues.

It has also been our experience that managers need to plan for continuous communication and coordination. For example, once training has begun and participants have access to hardware and software, the most effective way to support utilization is to provide for regular communication among users. Since peers are likely to be functioning at a variety of levels in terms of microcomputer knowledge and sophistication, teachers can learn from one another through modeling and social reinforcement. It is also important to plan for communication and collaboration with regular educators. The use of microcomputing in special education may sometimes precede a similar level of use in regular classrooms, and this may result in resentment and misunderstanding. The microcomputer has the potential for serving as an important bridge between regular education and special services programs.

A further conclusion is that there needs to be a continuum of training alternatives for staff. The development and management of the human resources involved in the use of microcomputers is a most challenging problem. Teachers (and students) will progress at different rates, and take different paths, in their development. Some will acquire advanced programming skills and tailor software to their instructional needs, while others will rely on pre-established packages for this purpose. Still others will employ microcomputers more mechanically (and not necessarily ineffectively), through the exclusive use of commercially available material. Staff development needs to be guided by the evolving nature of the project and the needs of the people involved.

Finally, planners must explicitly determine the relationships between the microcomputer project and the instructional programs already in place. In programs where the curriculum is adequately specified, it will be easier to make linkages with commercial or locally developed software. When such linkages are not made at the outset, disorganization and eventual disillusion may result.

REFERENCES

American Psychological Association. (1974). *Standards for educational and psychological tests.* Washington, DC: American Psychological Association.

Davis, H., & Salasin, S. (1975). The utilization of evaluation. In E. Streunig & M. Guttentag (Ed.), *Handbook of evaluation research* (Vol. 1). Beverly Hills, CA: Sage.

Glaser, E. M., & Backer, T. E. (1980). Durability of innovations: How goal attainment scaling programs fare over time. *Community Mental Health Journal, 16,* 130-143.

Human Interaction Research Institute. (1976). *Putting knowledge to use: A distillation of the literature regarding knowledge transfer and change.* Los Angeles: Author.

Kiresuk, T. J. (1980). Organizational readiness for program evaluation. In R. J. Perloff (Ed.), *Evaluator interventions.* Beverly Hills, CA: Sage.

Miles, M. B. (1965). Planned change and organizational health: Figure and ground. In R. O. Carlson (Ed.), *Change processes in public schools.* Eugene, OR: University of Oregon.

National Science Foundation. (1973). *Science, technology and innovation.* Columbus, OH: Battelle Columbus Laboratories.

Taber, F. M. (1983). *Microcomputers in special education.* Reston, VA: Council for Exceptional Children.

Tuckman, B. W. (1972). *Conducting educational research.* New York: Harcourt Brace Jovanovich.

Using Microcomputers for Administrative Purposes: Suggestions for Development and Management

David L. Hayden

ABSTRACT. Microcomputers can serve a range of purposes in public schools including enhancing administration of special services. However, special services administrators at local and state levels perform a range of functions which involve diverse information-management needs. In this paper, ways that microcomputers may assist administration of special services are put forth. Then, considerations for local level special services administrators in developing and managing information systems are discussed, followed by similar discussion for state level administrators.

Special services administrators have diverse, often changing and sometimes unanticipated information-management needs. Microcomputer systems offer the potential to help manage information more effectively as well as to improve productivity.

This paper is based on past experience of the author in implementing a computer assisted management system for administrators and direct service providers. The system connects the local education agency (LEA) to the computer system operated by the Maryland State Department of Education. The state Special Service Information System (SSIS) is 12 years old and the school-based microcomputer Special Education Management System (SEMS) has been in

---

Request for reprints should be sent to: David L. Hayden, Division of Special Education, Maryland State Department of Education, 200 Baltimore Street, Baltimore, Maryland 21201.

© 1984 by The Haworth Press, Inc. All rights reserved.

operation for five years (Maryland State Department of Education, 1982, 1983). Drawing on this experience, this paper describes some of the uses to which information management systems can be put and offers suggestions for the development and management of microcomputers used by LEA and state education agency (SEA) managers.

WAYS MICROCOMPUTERS CAN ASSIST ADMINISTRATION

At the state level, a Special Services Information System (SSIS) can be used to compile information on the numbers of special needs children in the state, their special education needs, the services they receive, and the number of staff providing these services. The state can use the SSIS as a major source of information to meet its planning, monitoring, and accounting responsibilities for special education. Information from the SSIS can be used to monitor the special education services delivery system in each of the local public school districts, and in state-operated programs. The SSIS can be used to satisfy state and federal reporting requirements under the Education for All Handicapped Children Act (P.L. 94-142), as well as reporting requirements for Title VI and Title IX of the Civil Rights Act (as these Titles apply to special education), and Section 504 of the Rehabilitation Act of 1973.

At the LEA level, a computer-based management system increases the value of program information and reduces duplication in data collection and staff time. The system typically produces reports that help administrators monitor resource allocation and services provided students, maintain staff records, and plan facilities' utilization across schools within the LEA.

In addition to performing tasks relevant to central administration, microcomputers can be used by LEA staff to assist in the management of instruction. Microcomputers can provide a flexible structure for indexing materials and strategies, linking criterion-referenced tests to curriculum objectives, and matching objectives across various courses. These systems can also be used in monitoring the selection of objectives by direct service staff for various types of handicapped students (Hayden, 1983; Riswen, 1979) to determine what general goals are being set for different populations of students.

DEVELOPING AND MANAGING INFORMATION SYSTEMS: SOME CONSIDERATIONS FOR LEA ADMINISTRATORS

For microcomputers to be effectively used in special education administration, LEA administrators must play a leadership role in planning for and creating a supportive environment. Some suggestions for creating such an environment follow:

1. *Establish a General Policy.* Administrators can force the district to utilize new technology, constrain the use of technology, or adopt a neutral policy which is neither forcing nor constraining. Forcing the technology can be advantageous because it places the LEA in an advanced position relative to other school districts. Jumping in early can lead to productivity gains that other districts will not realize. A forcing role is, however, a high risk endeavor because some of the early promise of microcomputer technology may not materialize as planned by manufacturers or staff. In addition, staff may react negatively if they perceive that technology is being forced upon them. By the same token, a policy of constraint will save resources and avoid many of the problems inherent in the utilization of new technology. It may, however, serve to prevent the district from operating in the most efficient way possible.

2. *Develop a Strategic Plan.* LEA administrators have two choices with regard to planning. They can focus on a strategic-use or on an acquisition level plan. At the strategic-use level, supervisors think through where the technology can be used to have the greatest impact on special education. Where, for example, can the technology be used to raise the overall quality of special education or reduce paper work in administration (e.g., a system for storing instructional objectives and test items that can be used by all teachers and direct service delivery staff)? At the acquisition level, administrators focus on individual instances in which new technology can contribute (e.g., a language device for use by nonverbal handicapped students). Planning at the strategic level has the potential for high pay-off in that it can create a critical mass of applications focusing on a specific problem.

3. *Identify the Classes of Users and Uses.* Professionals such as speech pathologists and psychologists may use microcomputers for such purposes as scoring or administering tests to individual students. This use of microcomputers is a personal one that does not require much standardization in the manner in which the machine is

used across users or machines; different psychologists may use the same machine for different purposes or different machines for different purposes without negatively affecting school district operations. On the other hand, special education administrators will often use the microcomputer in a more structured manner, as when the machine is used solely for maintaining student record information. Stand-alone unstructured uses require less central management and approval. Structured applications require more extensive planning efforts. These classes of users need to be thoroughly identified to provide a basis for coordinated management actions.

4. *Encourage Formation of Users Groups.* Many school staff members employ the same ideas, data, or programs in working with microcomputers. Establishing groups of users with common responsibilities promotes the sharing of ideas, as well as the development of new solutions to problems. User groups may also help to set equipment and software standards to facilitate the acquisition of common equipment and software that is compatible with that equipment.

5. *Establish a Support Structure.* Support structures need to be established across programs in every school. Such structures should be established as formal service groups to perform the following tasks:

—Help new users get started.
—Provide equipment repair and maintenance.
—Provide software clearing-house information and advice.
—Provide a hotline number to solve the problems of the user.
—Provide training to improve computer literacy throughout the LEA.

6. *Develop Data Rules.* Data rules should be built around an "ownership" concept which describes who owns the data stored in the management system. The responsibilities and rights of an owner also should be outlined. LEA staff, and especially special education staff, will need to develop rules on sharing, accessing, and updating data, and on who has authority to do what to what data. This is especially important when members of different departments use the same microcomputer. In these instances, many individuals have the potential to access special education student information. Because such information is confidential and access to it is protected by federal and state law, clear ownership rights must be established.

7. *Evaluate the Need for a User Telecommunications Network.* Telecommunications networks help school administrators to share data with other schools, other districts, and with county and state education agencies. Such data are shared by linking one computer to another over the telephone lines. Before developing a telecommunications network, LEA administrators should determine what the purpose of the network will be (e.g., sending SEMS data from schools to the LEA, and from the LEAs to the SEA); who will need to communicate with whom (e.g., the central district office and the SEA); what data will be exchanged (e.g., data on the number of children receiving special services by handicap); what type of communication facilities are available; and what devices must be used.

DEVELOPING INFORMATION MANAGEMENT SYSTEMS: SOME CONSIDERATIONS FOR STATE ADMINISTRATORS

Just as LEA administrators must take a leadership role to effectively implement information systems at the local level, state administrators have a similar obligation to provide direction and encouragement to the local school administrators in their state. Some suggestions for these administrators are:

1. *Develop a Fact Finding System.* Many decisions regarding microcomputer use will be decentralized decisions made by principals and education supervisors in the schools. To reach these managers, an *ongoing* special education microcomputer fact finding survey system should be planned and implemented so that the different administrative uses being made of microcomputers across the state can be identified.

2. *Promote a Joint Literacy Plan.* Almost all administrators at the school, LEA and state level will eventually need to understand microcomputers to effectively perform their jobs. State policy makers should plan to work with the SEA staff, LEA officials, institutions of higher education, and private technology training centers to consider the implementation of a staff development plan for the use of microcomputers in special education. A series of conferences might be used to help LEA special education directors understand the issues related to the use of microcomputers. These workshops might include content focusing on computer literacy for administrators at the LEA and state level, organizing for information management, establishing support structures, and on managing large numbers of low-cost microcomputers.

3. *Develop a Resource Guide and Catalog for LEA Microcomputer Users.* The resource guide and catalog should contain comparison information on computers and software packages being used for special education management in the state. The guide should assist the microcomputer novice in obtaining specific information needed to make sensible purchase decisions.

4. *Conduct Pilot Projects.* To help in the management and coordination of microcomputers, pilot projects should be established which focus on important issues (e.g., How is management information best shared with intermediate and state units?; How can technical support be most effectively provided to school district staff?). A series of seminars might be planned to ensure that the lessons learned through pilot efforts are communicated to school, LEA and state managers throughout the state.

5. *Develop Local Telecommunication Network Policies.* Data exchange policies should be established among schools and LEAs so that information can be easily exchanged across the telephone lines. Common procedures and data formats will facilitate the ready exchange of data among schools and LEAs and between LEAs and the SEA. In addition, common formats will permit data to be easily summarized across schools and districts.

6. *Establish an Evaluation Program.* Mechanisms should be established to gather information that can be used to document progress at the state level and to improve local level efforts to effectively use microcomputers in administration. Because state-operated technical support staff interact with school personnel across the state, technical support staff will be aware of common problems and successes. This information should be fed back to LEA staff so that they can benefit from the solutions others have found to common problems and avoid common pitfalls. An annual report of progress throughout the state and problems discovered across special education areas might be published as a means of sharing this information with those from other states.

CONCLUSION

Microcomputers present the potential to greatly improve the management of special education services. Generally accepted models for managing the use of microcomputers in special education administration, however, do not exist. For LEA and SEA administrators, the best strategy may be to carefully develop a specific plan for allocating microcomputers, managing their use, and evaluating their utility as administrative mechanisms for improving special programs (Airasian & Maudaus, 1983; Armstrong, 1979; Hayden, 1980). A specific management plan should provide direction to staff in how microcomputers are to be used as well as guidance to administrators in how their use should eventually be evaluated.

REFERENCES

Airasian, P. W., & Maudaus, G. F. (1983). Linking testing and instruction: Policy issues. *Journal of Educational Measurement, 20,* 103-118.

Armstrong J. (1979). A generalized model for the evaluation of instructional materials and media. In J. Armstrong (Ed.), *A source book for the evaluation of instructional materials and media.* Madison, Wisconsin: University of Wisconsin, Special Education Instructional Material Center.

Hayden, D. (1980). *Special education program evaluation: Resource manual.* Baltimore: Maryland State Department of Education.

Hayden, D., Palmer, T., & Mark, D. (1983). Personal computer applications for the learning disabled: Managing instructional materials. *Journal of Learning Disabilities, 11,* 83-97.

Maryland State Department of Education. (1982). Special service information system: Manual of instructions. Baltimore: Author.

Maryland State Department of Education. (1983). Computer assisted management of individualized education program for teachers—User manual. Baltimore: Author.

259607